The Responsibility of Intellectuals

The Responsibility of Intellectuals

Reflections by Noam Chomsky and others after 50 years

Edited by
Nicholas Allott, Chris Knight and Neil Smith

First published in 2019 by
UCL Press
University College London
Gower Street
London WC1E 6BT

Available to download free: www.ucl.ac.uk/ucl-press

ISBN: 978-1-78735-553-8 (Hbk.)
ISBN: 978-1-78735-552-1 (Pbk.)
ISBN: 978-1-78735-551-4 (PDF)
ISBN: 978-1-78735-554-5 (epub)
ISBN: 978-1-78735-555-2 (mobi)
DOI: https://doi.org/10.14324/111.9781787355514

Contents

List of figures   vii

Contributors   viii

Preface   x

Introduction: 'The Responsibility of Intellectuals': what it
does and does not say   1
Nicholas Allott

Remarks on the historical context of the essay 'The
Responsibility of Intellectuals'   5
Noam Chomsky

1 Reflections on Chomsky's 'The Responsibility of Intellectuals'   7
   Neil Smith and Amahl Smith

2 'I don't want no peace'– a black, Jewish activist's take on the
   responsibility of intellectuals   26
   Jackie Walker

3 The responsibility of intellectuals in the era of bounded
   rationality and *Democracy for Realists*   32
   Nicholas Allott

4 The propaganda model and the British nuclear weapons debate   45
   Milan Rai

5 Speaking truth to power – from within the heart of the empire   53
   Chris Knight

6 The abdication of responsibility   71
   Craig Murray

7 Replies and commentary   75
   Noam Chomsky

8 Conference Q&A   102
Noam Chomsky

Bibliography   121

Index   138

List of figures

Fig. 5.1 Jerome Wiesner (far left), the scientist who recruited
Chomsky to MIT, with Defense Secretary Robert
McNamara and Vice-President Lyndon Johnson in
the White House, 1961. (Courtesy of White House
Photographs. John F. Kennedy Presidential Library
and Museum, Boston. Photo: Abbie Rowe)   64

Fig. 5.2 Preparation for nuclear war: the SAGE (Semi-
Automatic Ground Environment) air defense system.
In the 1960s, the Pentagon sponsored linguists in
the hope of making such computer systems easier
to use. (Photo: Andreas Feininger/The LIFE Picture
Collection/Getty Images)   64

Fig. 5.3 Protesters demonstrate outside one of MIT's nuclear
missile laboratories, November 1969. (Courtesy of
MIT Museum, Cambridge, MA)   65

Fig. 5.4 Police disperse protesters, November 1969. (Courtesy
of MIT Museum, Cambridge, MA)   65

Fig. 5.5 Building the US nuclear stockpile: General James
McCormack (in uniform), a future vice-president at
MIT, next to Robert Oppenheimer (second on the
left), on the way to Los Alamos, 1947. (Photo: US
Dept of Energy, Washington, DC)   66

Fig. 5.6 Former MIT Provost, and future Director of the CIA,
John Deutch at the Pentagon. (Photo: James E.
Jackson, 12 April 1993. US Department of Defense,
Washington, DC. The appearance of US Department
of Defense (DoD) visual information does not imply or
constitute DoD endorsement)   66

Contributors

Noam Chomsky is Institute Professor Emeritus at the Massachusetts Institute of Technology and laureate professor at the University of Arizona, and probably the most prominent linguist in history. His ideas have revolutionised the study of language and have had a profound impact on psychology, philosophy and intellectual life more broadly. He is also a longstanding political activist and leading critic of US foreign policy. His political work includes many books, hundreds of articles, and countless speeches, interviews, letters and emails.

Nicholas Allott is senior lecturer in English language at the University of Oslo. Previously he has been research fellow at CSMN, University of Oslo, and a teaching fellow at UCL, where he completed his PhD in linguistics in 2008. His research interests include pragmatics, semantics of natural languages, legal language and interpretation, and philosophy of linguistics. He is co-author of *Chomsky: Ideas and Ideals* (Cambridge University Press, 2016).

Chris Knight is a research fellow at UCL, a longstanding political activist and the author of *Blood Relations: Menstruation and the Origins of Culture* (Yale University Press, 1995) and *Decoding Chomsky: Science and Revolutionary Politics* (Yale University Press, 2016). He is co-founder of EVOLANG, the interdisciplinary conference series on the evolution of language, and has co-edited several books on human cultural origins.

Craig Murray is a writer and activist. He is the author of *Murder in Samarkand* (Mainstream Publishing, 2006) and other non-fiction best-sellers, and was the Rector of Dundee University. He became well known to the public when he resigned as British ambassador to Uzbekistan in protest against British collusion with the Uzbek dictatorship during the 'war on terror'. For this act of whistleblowing, he received the Sam Adams Award for Integrity in Intelligence in 2006.

Milan Rai is a longstanding anti-war activist and writer. He is the author of several books including *Chomsky's Politics* (Verso, 1995), the only monograph on the subject, and *7/7: The London Bombings, Islam and the Iraq War* (Pluto, 2006). He has been co-editor of *Peace News* since 2007.

Amahl Smith is a charity finance director. He is a former treasurer of Amnesty International UK and of the Business and Human Rights Resource Centre.

Neil Smith is emeritus professor of linguistics at UCL. His first career was as an Africanist and from 1964 to 1972 he was Lecturer in West African languages at London's School of Oriental and African Studies. He was then appointed head of linguistics at UCL, a position he kept until his retirement in 2006. He is best known for his research on first language acquisition, especially the acquisition of phonology; for his investigation over many years into the remarkable abilities of a polyglot savant, Christopher; and for his work on Chomsky. He is co-author of *Chomsky: Ideas and Ideals* (Cambridge University Press, 2016) and has also written a number of books of essays popularising linguistics.

Jackie Walker is a black, Jewish activist and author, a founding member of Jewish Voice for Labour, a defender of Palestinian rights, a long-standing campaigner against racism and the former Vice-Chair of Momentum, the left-wing movement in the British Labour Party. Author of the acclaimed family memoir *Pilgrim State* (Sceptre, 2008), she has recently staged a one-woman show, *The Lynching*, designed to combat racism – including antisemitism – in certain sectors of British political life. Like Chomsky, Walker has been criticised for voicing perspectives on Israel and aspects of Jewish history that prominent supporters of Israel have described as controversial or even antisemitic. In 2016, allegations of this kind, which Walker strongly rejects, led to her suspension from the Labour Party. Chomsky is one of a number of Jewish intellectuals to have lent public support to her campaign to be reinstated.

Preface

With the publication of 'The Responsibility of Intellectuals' in the *New York Review of Books* in February 1967, Noam Chomsky burst onto the US political scene as a leading critic of the war in Vietnam. The essay was then republished many times, starting with its inclusion in Chomsky's first political book, *American Power and the New Mandarins*, in 1969. 'The Responsibility of Intellectuals' has aptly been described as 'the single most influential piece of anti-war literature' of the Vietnam period.[1]

By the late 1960s, Chomsky had been involved in the nascent anti-war movement for some time. But until the essay appeared he was known to the wider public, if at all, only for his ground-breaking work in linguistics. Since then, Chomsky has been a leading public intellectual, publishing hundreds of essays and dozens of books and giving thousands of talks and interviews. By 2004, even the *New York Times* – not the greatest fan of Chomsky's political writings – had to admit that 'if book sales are any standard to go by, he may be the most widely read American voice on foreign policy on the planet today'.[2]

Chomsky's political commentary has ranged from US wars in Indochina, Latin America and the Middle East to analyses of western political and economic policy more broadly. He is also known for his work on the special role of the media in modern democracies, how they 'manufacture consent' by keeping certain views and topics off the agenda. All of this political activity has taken place in parallel with Chomsky's work as a linguist at the Massachusetts Institute of Technology where he revolutionised the study of language and the mind, rehabilitating the study of mental structure with a profound impact not only on linguistics but also on psychology and philosophy.

This book revisits 'The Responsibility of Intellectuals' half a century on and celebrates Chomsky's life of activism. It includes six new essays written to celebrate Chomsky's famous intervention. The authors were all inspired by the theme of the responsibility of intellectuals but their contributions are very varied. Some have been studying Chomsky's thought for years, others write about their own personal experiences of the price paid for speaking out.

The book has three contributions from Chomsky. He briefly explains the background to the original publication of 'The Responsibility of Intellectuals'. He also provides replies to the other contributors, with extensive commentary on issues that they raise. Finally, there is wide-ranging discussion from a question-and-answer session he conducted in February 2017 on the 50th anniversary of the publication of his essay.[3]

The preparation of this book has taken longer than we had anticipated and has led us to incur a number of debts of gratitude. The most important of these is obviously to Noam Chomsky himself and to his wife Valéria Wasserman Chomsky. Despite the considerable pressures of the various strands of his life, he made time to join us for a lengthy question-and-answer session via video link in UCL, and then reacted to the issues raised in the papers; he and Valéria replied to questions and dealt with many problems, always with grace and patience at a time when they were relocating to Arizona.

For financial support we are grateful to the British Academy, especially to its past president Nick Stern (Baron Stern of Brentford), and to UCL, whose Department of Anthropology and Division of Psychology and Language Sciences gave generous subventions. We are similarly indebted to UCL's audiovisual unit for organising with flawless efficiency the video link with Arizona.

We also want to express our appreciation to UCL Press for their positive reaction to our often importunate questions and requests. Lara Speicher in particular has been helpful beyond the call of duty, and Laura Morley and Jaimee Biggins have done wonderful jobs as copy editor and Managing Editor respectively.

A number of other individuals should be mentioned for their contribution to one or other aspect of the enterprise. They include all the contributors but also Jui Chu Hsu Allott, Elliot Murphy and Kriszta Szendrői.

Nicholas Allott, Chris Knight and Neil Smith

Notes

1   David Schalk, *War and the Ivory Tower: Algeria and Vietnam* (Oxford: Oxford University Press, 1991), 141–2.
2   Samantha Power, 'The everything explainer,' *New York Times*, 4 January 2004.
3   On 25 February 2017, the editors of this volume held a conference at UCL entitled 'The Responsibility of Intellectuals – 50 Years On'. The essays by Jackie Walker, Milan Rai, Chris Knight and Craig Murray and the introduction by Nicholas Allott are based, to varying degrees, on the talks presented at this conference. Videos of all the talks, and the lively Q&As, can be found at http://scienceandrevolution.org/blog/noam-chomskys-the-responsibility-of-intellectuals-50-years-on and on the UCL website, at http://mediacentral.ucl.ac.uk/Play/5830 and ... /5831, /5832, /5833, /5834, /5835, /5836, /5837, /5838, /5839, /5840

Introduction
'The Responsibility of Intellectuals': what it does and does not say

Nicholas Allott

Chomsky's classic essay is an attack on experts, technocrats and intellectuals of all kinds who serve the interests of the powerful by lying, by producing propaganda or by providing 'pseudo-scientific justifications for the crimes of the state' (as Jay Parini recently put it).[1] Of course, unlike certain recently prominent politicians on both sides of the Atlantic, Chomsky has nothing against experts as such. What he argues is that they are not morally exceptional.

He wrote in the essay: 'It is the responsibility of intellectuals to speak the truth and to expose lies.' As he said, this is, or should be, truistic. It's just obvious that intellectuals should tell the truth. It is equally obvious that it is not only intellectuals who have this responsibility. But Chomsky argues that intellectuals have responsibilities that go beyond the responsibilities of others because they have a particularly privileged position. He wrote:

> For a privileged minority, Western democracy provides the leisure, the facilities, and the training to seek the truth lying hidden behind the veil of distortion and misrepresentation, ideology and class interest, through which the events of current history are presented to us.[2]

As Chomsky has pointed out many times since, those of us living in relatively free societies have considerable advantages. We can express our opinions in public without the fear of being put in prison or tortured for doing so. It follows that we have the responsibility to speak out about injustice. But within our society there are some people who have further advantages and privileges: training in reading texts critically, looking up sources and so on, and the time and job security to be able to do so in the sustained way that it takes to expose the lies of the state and other powerful agents. These are the people to whom Chomsky referred as intellectuals. The now unfashionable label shouldn't distract us from his point: because of their advantages and privileges they have a correspondingly weightier responsibility.

It is also worth pointing out that Chomsky did not say – and did not mean to imply – that this is their only responsibility or that it always outweighs all others. We all have a lot of responsibilities! As he explained in response to criticism of the essay, it is easy to imagine more or less extreme situations in which the responsibility to tell the truth is outweighed by other obligations. But still, it is an important, central responsibility. As he said at the time in a reply to critics:

> Surely everyone understands that there are no simple formulas that determine proper behavior in all conceivable situations. But from this it does not follow, surely, that one must abandon all concern for standards and general values.[3]

All this may seem perfectly obvious. Why was it worth saying? Why is it worth saying again now? One reason is that so many public figures are happy to lie and propagandise, now, as back then, and the reaction, or rather the lack of it, suggests that we do not always take seriously the responsibility to tell the truth. Chomsky provides numerous examples in his essay, across the US party political spectrum, from Henry Kissinger (a Republican and foreign policy 'hawk') to Arthur Schlesinger (a Democratic activist known as a 'dove').

Schlesinger was a famous academic historian who, while working as an adviser to President Kennedy in 1961, lied to the press about the attempted US 'Bay of Pigs' invasion of Cuba, as he later blandly admitted. As Chomsky said, what is interesting about this isn't so much 'that one man is quite happy to lie in behalf of a cause which he knows to be unjust; but ... that such events provoke so little response in the intellectual community.'

In the essay Chomsky sets out one of the enduring themes of his political critique of US foreign policy, scepticism about American exceptionalism: the idea that the US, unlike other powerful states, is essentially benevolent. As he shows, there are close historical parallels for US rhetoric:

In 1784, the British Parliament announced: 'To pursue schemes of conquest and extension of dominion in India are measures repugnant to the wish, honour, and policy of this nation.' Shortly after this, the conquest of India was in full swing.[4]

This – which is incidentally a good example of one of the other hallmarks of Chomsky's political writing, biting sarcasm about injustice – should bring to mind John Stuart Mill,[5] surely one of the most important and wide-ranging philosophers, described by a leading modern expert as 'a "public moralist" and public intellectual *par excellence*'.[6] He worked for the East India Company for most of his adult life – a criminal enterprise if ever there was one – and argued in favour of what he regarded as benevolent (British) 'despotism' in India and elsewhere as

> a legitimate mode of government in dealing with barbarians [sic] provided the end is their improvement and the means justified by actually effecting that end.[7]

That attitude would be bad enough if the goal really were the 'improvement' of those subjugated, as Mill may have piously hoped, but history suggests that the goals of the powerful are consistently more self-serving, and the effects of their actions less pleasant for those under their power, from the Athenian invasion of Melos to the US wars in Asia in the 1960s and today. As Chomsky has repeatedly shown, if you want to know the overriding aims of the powerful you have to look at their actions – as well as internal memos and other documents not intended for public consumption – and not be taken in by rhetoric.

There is another reason that we need reminding of the truisms in Chomsky's essay. In the face of the temptation not to make a fuss, not to rock the boat and not to endanger one's livelihood, it is almost always easier to serve the interests of the powerful, or to say and do nothing, than it is to stand up for what is right by speaking out.

Chomsky has been speaking out now for more than 50 years, and his work has been an unparalleled resource and inspiration for those of us who want to see through lies and propaganda and understand the world, so that we can change it for the better. His work and the example he sets should continue to inspire us.

Notes

1   Noam Chomsky, 'The responsibility of intellectuals,' *New York Review of Books*, 23 February 1967; Jay Parini, 'Noam Chomsky's "Responsibility of Intellectuals" after 50 years: It's an even heavier responsibility now,' *Salon*, 11 February 2017.
2   Noam Chomsky, *American Power and the New Mandarins* (New York: Vintage Books, 1969), 323.
3   Noam Chomsky, 'Reply to critics,' *New York Review of Books*, 20 April 1967.
4   Noam Chomsky, *American Power and the New Mandarins* (New York: Vintage Books, 1969), 356–7.
5   This short essay started as a talk introducing Chomsky and other speakers at UCL. J.S. Mill attended lectures at UCL, which was founded by (among others) his father James Mill, also a utilitarian philosopher, as a secular, liberal alternative to Oxbridge.
6   Georgios Varouxakis, quoted in UCL, 'UCL marks a place in British intellectual history for John Stuart Mill,' press release, 23 March 2006, https://www.ucl.ac.uk/media/library/mill
7   For the quotation from Mill, and discussion of his career at the East India Company, see: Abram L. Harris, 'John Stuart Mill: Servant of the East India Company,' *The Canadian Journal of Economics and Political Science/ Revue Canadienne d'Economique et de Science Politique* 30, no. 2 (1964), 191. For a recent overview of the British Empire's attitude towards and effects on India, see Jon Wilson, *India Conquered: Britain's Raj and the Chaos of Empire* (London: Simon & Schuster, 2016).

Remarks on the historical context of the essay 'The Responsibility of Intellectuals'

Noam Chomsky

These remarks are from a conference held at UCL on 25 February 2017. The event commemorated the 50th anniversary of the publication of 'The Responsibility of Intellectuals'.

Let me give a little bit of the background. The essay itself was really a talk given in early 1966, about a year before it appeared, to a student group at Harvard University, which published a student journal. The journal was *Mosaic*, the periodical – believe it or not – of the Harvard Hillel Society. This was pre-1967, and things were very different. This was one of a constant stream of talks, often many a day, to all kinds of audiences. It began pretty much when John F. Kennedy escalated the war in Vietnam in 1961–62.

Since this talk happened to be at Harvard, it was particularly important to focus on intellectual elites and their relation to government. The reason was that the Harvard faculty was quite prominent in the Kennedy and Johnson administrations. The National Security Advisor, McGeorge Bundy, was a former dean at Harvard; many other faculty were either in the administration or travelled back regularly from Cambridge to Washington. And the spirit of Camelot reigned at Harvard – as in fact it still does. That was the reason for the particular focus of the talk, different from other talks at the time.

I should perhaps say something about the general context. This was Cambridge, in the Boston area, probably the most liberal city in the United States, and you can get a picture of what things were like by two events that had just taken place: one about the time of the talk, one a couple of months earlier. October 1965 was the first planned international day of protest against the Vietnam War, and of course the anti-war activists in Boston wanted to participate in it. So we arranged a demonstration at the Boston Common – essentially the equivalent of Hyde Park, the standard place for public meetings. I was supposed to be one of the speakers. The crowd gathered, but the event never really took place. It was broken up violently by counter-demonstrators. You couldn't hear the speakers. Real violence was prevented by a big police appearance. The demonstrations – not just in Boston – were bitterly condemned by congressional liberals. The demonstrators were regarded as traitors. How dare they ask these questions! The *Boston Globe*, probably the most liberal paper in the country, devoted almost the entire front page to condemning the demonstrators. That was the general mood.

The next international day of protest was in March 1966, about the time when this talk was given at Harvard. We realised we couldn't have a public demonstration, it would be broken up violently. So we decided to have a meeting instead at the Arlington Street Church in downtown Boston. The church was attacked – tomatoes, tin cans, and so on. Again, a police presence prevented greater violence. That was the context at the time that this was being given.

Well, despite quite overwhelming opposition, the small number of anti-war activists were proceeding at that time well beyond talks and organising efforts. In March 1965, a year earlier, we had tried to organise a national tax resistance campaign. It was mostly based at MIT, in fact, at the laboratory where I was working, the Research Laboratory of Electronics. By 1966, there were the beginnings of efforts to organise a national resistance organisation, called 'Resist'. It became public in October 1967, and by 1968 it was the target of the first government trials of the resistance. And again, MIT was pretty much the academic centre, the same lab for the most part.

In February 1967, the *New York Review of Books* did publish the article that had appeared in the Harvard student journal, edited with expanded footnotes and so on. And that was followed, once in the journal, by interchanges and discussions on moving from protest to direct resistance, which by then was pretty much underway. By late 1967, there was a large-scale, popular anti-war movement finally taking shape – much too late, but quite significant in scale and with long-term consequences. That's the general context in which the article appeared in the *New York Review*.

1

Reflections on Chomsky's 'The Responsibility of Intellectuals'

Neil Smith and Amahl Smith

Introduction

Chomsky set out three responsibilities of intellectuals in his classic paper: to speak the truth and expose lies; to provide historical context; and to lift the veil of ideology, the underlying framework of ideas that limits the boundaries of debate.[1]

As documented extensively in the press, there is ample evidence from Trump's tweets in the US and the disinformation put about in the UK Brexit referendum that the incidence of lying on the part of the powerful has not decreased and the need to speak truth has not gone away. These examples might give the impression that there's no need for intellectuals in general 'to speak the truth and to expose lies', as mainstream journalists will do it anyway. But in these cases there are powerful (indeed elite) forces on both sides, and it is generally only by the actions of individual intellectuals that the facts are revealed and discussed.

The archetypal example is Edward Snowden, an employee of the NSA (National Security Agency) who leaked vast numbers of classified documents to journalists, revealing the massive surveillance of its own citizens perpetrated by the US government. His action was condemned as treachery by some, lauded as heroic patriotism by others. Explaining what drove him to act as he did, Snowden said that 'the breaking point was seeing the Director of National Intelligence, James Clapper, directly lie under oath to Congress'.[2] Chomsky commended Snowden's behaviour, saying 'he should be welcomed as a person who carried out the obligations of a citizen. He informed American citizens of what their government is doing to them. That's exactly what a person who has real patriotism ... would do.'[3]

Clearly, the veil of ideology still hangs heavy and historical context is often lacking, as is evident from the current debate on what to do about North Korea or the ongoing problems in the Middle East. Sadly, Chomsky's paper 'The Responsibility of Intellectuals' (hereafter RoI) is as relevant today as it was 50 years ago. Much, however, has changed in the intervening period, and it is worth exploring how these changes have affected – and perhaps subtly changed – the responsibilities of intellectuals.

At a minimum, there have been changes in the number, nature and status of intellectuals; the people to whom truth needs to be spoken; and what else is required if speaking truth and exposing lies is to have any impact. One is responsible for the foreseeable consequences of one's actions; if there are no consequences, when should one persevere and when should one stop wasting one's time and do something more effective? Moreover, technological advances have complicated the landscape. We explore each of these issues.

The number, nature and status of intellectuals

As Dwight Macdonald made clear in the articles from which Chomsky drew his inspiration,[4] all people have a moral and political duty to speak truth to power but – as Chomsky emphasises – the combination of training, facilities, political liberty, access to information and freedom of expression enjoyed by some intellectuals imposes deeper responsibilities on them. While it may not always be obvious who counts as an intellectual for these purposes, what is clear is that the number of intellectuals has increased dramatically over the last 50 years, as exemplified in the UK by the huge expansion of university education over that period: from less than 10 per cent of the population to nearly 50 per cent. Disappointingly, only a minority of these new intellectuals see themselves as 'value-oriented' (in Chomsky's more recent terminology). The contrast is between 'technocratic and policy-oriented intellectuals' (the 'good guys', in the eyes of the establishment, who merely serve external power) and the 'value-oriented intellectuals' (the 'bad guys', from an establishment perspective, who engage in critical analysis and 'delegitimation').[5] This sardonic description characterises those who have a 'moral responsibility as decent human beings ... to advance the causes of freedom, justice, mercy, peace ... [as opposed to] ... the role they are expected to play, serving ... leadership and established institutions'.[6] Why the pernicious persistence of this distinction? There are many factors at play.

Intellectual courage

A significant factor in determining the preparedness of intellectuals to adopt a dissident stance is obviously fear of the consequences. As Craig Murray argues in his contribution to this book, the scope of academic freedom has declined significantly in the last few decades; universities are now expected to function as corporations, tenure is shrinking and funding has become short-term and dependent on continual measurement of research outputs, putting the funders in de facto academic and intellectual control.[7]

One concrete effect of this development can be seen in the casualisation of labour in academic life. The situation is worst for post-docs, who tend to get a sequence of short-term contracts with no career structure and little prospect of tenure.[8] The attendant insecurity is a powerful disincentive to say or do anything that might rock the boat – or irritate the representatives of big business that increasingly populate university governing bodies.

The increasing emphasis by a dominant bureaucracy on 'paper trails' (in some institutions faculty are enjoined to keep a written record of every interaction with any student, as a defence against possible later litigation) may also remove time and inclination to engage, as well as having a stultifying effect on intellectual development – perhaps accounting in part for the unprecedented discontent among staff, as demonstrated in the February to April 2018 widespread strike action involving some 65 universities.

For one prominent class of intellectuals (viz. academics), these developments have undoubtedly led to changes in their status and their ability – or courage – to undertake the analysis required to 'seek the truth lying hidden behind the veil of distortion and misrepresentation'. When one considers the situation of black intellectuals, then the issues, as Jackie Walker points out in her contribution, are all the more marked.[9] When historical injustices against black people remain barely acknowledged, let alone commemorated, it is with trepidation that people of colour raise their heads above the parapet to speak truth to power on any issue, even those that relate to their own history and experience.

Intellectual confidence

Even among those willing to face the consequences, lack of confidence, combined with the sneaking suspicion that what they do is ineffectual, discourages many from activism. It is interesting in this regard to contrast the paucity of 'intellectuals' in Chomsky's recent sense with the rise in the number of academics willing to step into the public eye to popularise their own subject, or just their own work. Alan Lightman draws contrasts between three levels of intellectual: those who speak and write for the public exclusively about their own discipline; those who speak and write about their discipline and how it relates to the social, cultural and political world; and those who contribute 'by invitation only': intellectuals who have become elevated to symbols and are asked to write and speak about public issues not necessarily connected to their original field of expertise at all.[10] The stock example is Einstein. Lightman then lists other people he would place in this category, beginning with Chomsky. Lightman's taxonomy cross-cuts Chomsky's, but his perception that a certain status should arise 'by invitation only' suggests that he has been seduced by the thought that speaking out on matters of public concern requires special authority. As Chomsky was at pains to point out, no special expertise or authority is required, and the responsibility to speak out rests with every one of us. It is not a matter of waiting to be invited, as this attitude encourages a kind of defeatism: if I'm not in the select group of 'invitees' what I do is irrelevant.

We have no easy solutions to the problems of intellectual courage and confidence, but the practical question of what can be done to encourage more people to do something – anything – on the kinds of issue featured in RoI is pressing.

The people to whom truth needs to be spoken

The responsibility of intellectuals is often summarised as 'speaking truth to power'. But it needs emphasising that speaking truth to power may not be the highest priority. Even where it is, the powers to which truth needs to be spoken are perhaps more disparate than before.

Speaking truth to the powerless

Those in power are often fully aware of what they are doing and why they are doing it. This is a point Chomsky has made forcefully about people like Churchill, who is cited in RoI as saying 'The government of the world must be entrusted to satisfied nations'. More generally, the elite need an accurate idea of what is going on in order to govern. Some of course may be (wilfully) ignorant, and it is necessary to speak truth to such people so that they cannot claim not to know the truth. But arguably the most important priority is to speak truth to the powerless, and to make apparently powerless people aware that, *in conjunction with others*, they need not remain powerless. David Hume recognised this in his 1741 maxim that 'power is in the hands of the governed'.[11] The first requirement, then, is to make such people aware of the true situation and hence of the possibility of their helping to bring about change.

Filling the gaps

Equally important is the fact that the responsibility to speak the truth has many facets: it is frequently not merely about exposing lies but about filling the gaps left, through calculation or inadvertence, by the mainstream media and the government agencies that feed them.[12] After the surprise result of the Brexit referendum it was striking that in her letter triggering the UK's actual departure the Prime Minister Theresa May made no mention of vexatious problems such as the status of Gibraltar, the fate of the fishing industry, the future of farmers and so on. It is impossible to cover every difficulty, but omissions give as clear an indication of policy priorities as do commitments. Similarly, in the 77-page government white paper (Cm 9417 – The United Kingdom's exit from and new partnership with the European Union) there is no mention of equalities or 'inequalities', such as the status of women. The problem of validity that these omissions raise is summed up in Sophie Chappell's aptly entitled paper 'Political deliberation under conditions of deception: The case of Brexit'.[13]

There are nonetheless some powers to whom it is necessary to speak the truth and, just as there have been changes in the nature of intellectuals, there have been changes in the powers to which truth needs to be spoken and the lies of which need to be exposed. RoI dealt almost exclusively with governments, but one needs now increasingly to look at companies and other non-state actors such as the public relations industry and the business community more generally, the National Rifle Association (NRA)[14] or Breitbart News.

With non-state actors, it is worth asking whether the nature of the responsibilities of intellectuals changes slightly. A significant omission from RoI is the contrary of exposing lies: applauding truth-telling or the defence of human rights. The effectiveness of speaking truth to governments is dubious, and praising them is generally irrelevant. Is either activity more efficacious when confronting corporate power?

Speaking truth to business

Despite the rise of fair trade initiatives, the single motivating factor for most companies remains profit, and companies are increasingly exploiting 'Strategic Lawsuits against Public Participation' (SLAPPs)[15] to inhibit intellectuals and organisations from campaigning against them. As a result, confronting business requires some changes in tactics. The Business and Human Rights Resource Centre (BHRRC)[16] provides useful examples and evidence, and there are some clear indicators of the effectiveness of both positive praise and negative criticism. Consider two examples: Uber and Penzeys Spices.

Both cases concerned the association of companies with (or against) the policies of US President Trump. In his campaign for the American presidency, Trump exhibited systematic Islamophobia, on one typical occasion issuing a statement demanding 'a total and complete shutdown of Muslims entering the United States'.[17] Soon after taking office he issued an executive order banning all refugees and people arriving from seven Muslim-majority countries (Chad, Iran, Iraq, Libya, Somalia, Syria and Yemen). The order was challenged in the courts, a revised version was issued (with Iraq omitted), and further modifications were made until the Supreme Court ruled in the President's favour. The (attempted) ban polarised the nation, with one significant side-effect being a strike by New York taxi drivers (many of whom are Muslims). An advertisement by Uber (a peer-to-peer ride-sharing company) that they were still 'open for business' was widely interpreted as an attempt to undermine the taxi drivers' strike action, and led to the social media campaign #DeleteUber, resulting in 200,000 people deleting their Uber accounts within days.[18] This is a good example of negative criticism of a business for its human rights stance having a significant (even if temporary) effect.

The converse situation is illustrated by the case of Penzeys Spice Company. The CEO attacked Trump's racist position on immigration in the company newsletter. This provoked a storm of heated reactions but, overall, had a huge (positive) impact on business.[19] Even if this was mainly rewarding 'anti-Trump' behaviour rather than pro-human rights behaviour, the strategy clearly influenced consumers, as witness headlines in the press such as 'CEO Bill Penzey Jr. is learning firsthand how blasting President Donald Trump is good for his bottom line'. Here admiration for a company's stance had a positive impact on its commercial performance.[20]

It is significant that hostility to Trump was crucial in determining the outcome of both examples and it would be foolish to draw too strong a conclusion; nevertheless, it is worth considering whether, at least in the case of businesses, there is a responsibility not just to expose lies but publicly to applaud those who take a positive stand.

Evidence for the effectiveness of activism?

There is a more general lesson about potential change to be learned from such examples. Chomsky has frequently spoken of improvements over time in the civic situation. In a conversation with Harry Belafonte he reports 'tremendous progress', saying that 'the country has become much more civilized in the last 50 or 60 years', citing women's rights, civil rights more generally, gay rights, environmental concerns, opposition to aggression, and so on.[21] If such historical evaluation is accurate it suggests that activist pressure can lead to change, providing some minimal grounds for optimism. Chomsky's own optimism is part of a deliberate strategy. He has often quoted Gramsci's aphorism 'you should have pessimism of the intellect and optimism of the will'.[22] Only the latter, Chomsky writes, protects you from the despair engendered by Trump's policies on the environment, described as a 'death knell for the human species'.[23]

Disseminating the truth

Value-oriented intellectuals wishing to speak the truth have greater difficulty than before in doing so in a way that can have any impact. There are several different issues at play.

Relativist views of truth

Since Chomsky wrote RoI there has been a rise within the academy of a kind of post-modernist relativism that questions whether there is an objective truth to be spoken (to power or otherwise), holding instead that different truths obtain for different groups.[24] There are good reasons to reject post-modernist relativism (see e.g. the books on the subject by the philosophers Thomas Nagel and Paul Boghossian), as Chomsky himself clearly does (as demonstrated in the 1971 debate between Chomsky and Foucault).[25] However its influence – and potentially its contribution to the current 'post truth' environment – cannot be ignored. While many who hold such views appear to be motivated (at least in part) by a desire to 'protect oppressed cultures from the charge of holding false or unjustified views', as Boghossian puts it,[26] such relativism is likely to inhibit criticism where criticism is due (e.g. the treatment of women in many Islamic states, or autocratic practices in non-western cultures). Moreover, it risks leaving the powerful immune to criticism: if the powerful can't criticise the oppressed – because different truths apply to them – presumably the oppressed can't criticise the powerful for the same reason. It is hard to gauge the significance of relativist views in this context but they may well have left some intellectuals disinclined to speak out and blunted the influence of those who have.

Such relativist views have plausibly also contributed to the rise of identity politics and the 'political correctness' that often accompanies them – including a disturbing increase in calls for 'no-platforming' at events held within academic institutions.[27] While it is undoubtedly true that charges of political correctness have often been used by those on the political right to divert attention from discriminatory behaviour against disadvantaged groups by mocking left-wing concerns with the language used and the impact on oppressed groups, it is also true that many of the left's behaviours have been counter-productive and have facilitated a rise in 'right-wing political correctness' which, as Paul Krugman pointed out,[28] 'unlike the liberal version – has lots of power and money behind it. And the goal is very much the kind of thing Orwell tried to convey with his notion of Newspeak: to make it impossible to talk, and possibly even think, about ideas that challenge the established order.'

Anti-intellectualism and distrust of experts

Even where intellectuals are prepared to speak out, the rise of anti-intellectualism makes it difficult for them to be heard.[29] As discussed above, Chomsky often emphasises the ways in which the 'political sciences' are used to obfuscate discussion and suggest that issues need to be left to 'the experts', pointing out that 'the cult of the experts is both self-serving, for those who propound it, and fraudulent'.[30] However, as Nichols has forcefully discussed, there is danger in embracing 'misguided intellectual egalitarianism'. 'Stubborn ignorance'[31] may result in countless deaths, as with the anti-vaccine campaign,[32] or in unexpected and unwanted electoral results. Nichols cites Michael Gove's interventions in the UK Brexit campaign[33] and Donald Trump's success in the American presidential election.[34]

One interesting development over the past 50 years is that with many of the issues most critical for human survival (e.g. climate change, nuclear proliferation, genetic engineering) the underlying moral and political issues are no more in need of 'expertise' than before. But there is now a 'hard science' dimension to understanding the issues and the options and a genuine need for people to understand some of the science. This has led to a situation where, deliberately or not, 'hard scientists' and not just 'political scientists' may use their expertise to exclude the general population from decision-making.

Take genetic engineering as an example. In evaluating whether to release a genetically modified organism it is obviously important to understand the science and the 'technical' risks in play. But it is also important to come back to the politics and economics as well. Many of those who oppose GM food, for example, do so not because they misunderstand the science but because they have concerns over the economics (where for example agribusinesses will hold patents over the GM seeds) or wider concerns over the political appropriateness of a technological solution at all. A more appropriate way of addressing the issue, one that leaves those most affected with control over their lives, might involve campaigning against the use of famine as a political tool, or working to eliminate waste in the supply chain.

Where Chomsky pointed to the fact that (policy) intellectuals liked their status as 'technical experts', there is a risk that hard scientists like their role in proposing technological solutions where these may not be what is politically or socially appropriate. The role of intellectuals in disentangling all this is more complicated now that it is not just a matter of seeing through the absurdities of political science but of patiently explaining the science one does need to know and its relevance to the moral and political issues. Intellectuals then need to show how those issues remain ones on which everyone (not just the experts) legitimately has an opinion and a responsibility to act. Large swathes of the population, including in particular those who voted for Trump, and those influenced by Michael Gove in the UK, now distrust so-called 'experts', including in particular scientific experts. As Gove (then Secretary of State for Justice, one of several cabinet portfolios he has held) put it: 'the people of this country have had enough of experts from organizations with acronyms saying that they know what is best'.[35] The root of the problem is then confusion (possibly created deliberately by politicians) about the role of experts and of scientific evidence in setting policy. It is only 'intellectuals' who can stand up for science while for many non-intellectuals science itself has fallen into disrepute. The upshot is that distrust of experts and the anti-intellectualism that accompanies it is making it harder for intellectuals to make the truth accessible to the powerless (because they won't listen to them) and may make it easier for the powerful to dismiss what they say when they speak truth to power.

The issues become more complex when the genetic engineering pertains to humans and the elimination of disease. It may seem apodictic that preventing Down syndrome or autism in the population is desirable, and that if that aim can be fulfilled there should be no disagreement about the morality of using genetic engineering to effect that goal. But the possibility of eliminating such conditions may be incompatible with maintaining due respect for people who have them. Many (high-functioning) autists consider autism to be not a disability but a difference to be celebrated. In that situation does the medical profession have the right to intervene? The same problem exists with greater clarity when it comes to eliminating deafness, as the Deaf community (with a capital D rather than lower-case d) is suspicious of or hostile to any such 'progress'.[36] There is no obviously correct answer here, but the history of eugenics indicates both that the issue is not quite as new as it might appear and, more importantly, the necessity for scrupulous respect for the scientific truth and the need to expose misrepresentation.

Social media

There have been radical changes in the outlets for disseminating information, whether true or false. On the one hand, there is ever greater corporate control of the media, which makes it harder for value-oriented intellectuals to find a mainstream platform; on the other hand, there is the rise of the internet and the dramatic increase in the influence of social media, which at least have the potential to provide platforms outside corporate control. Social media in particular can raise public awareness quickly, give a voice to the excluded, facilitate the persuasive impact of word of mouth, communicate a sense of urgency, allow safe communication under oppressive regimes and allow a sense of individual engagement and identification with an issue or a movement.[37] Despite this potential, the reality seems to be that for many people sources of news and opinion are getting narrower, with individuals retreating inside social media 'bubbles' where they are only fed news that reinforces their (establishment-influenced) beliefs and where the structure of news channels (tweets, Facebook feeds, etc.), with their emphasis on brevity, makes stepping outside the presuppositions of debate ever harder and providing historical context almost impossible.[38]

An important aspect of the rise of social media is the difficulty of knowing what lies are being propagated. Social media feeds can be targeted so finely it is hard to know what is being said to whom – lies are no longer always 'public', and you can't expose and correct what you don't know is being said: 'if you aren't a member of the community being served the lies, you're quite likely never to know that they are in circulation', as John Lanchester remarked in a chilling analysis of the pernicious effect of Facebook: 'in essence an advertising company which is indifferent to the content on its site'.[39]

Fake news

This issue is made more pressing by the vast increase in the number of ideologically motivated organisations deliberately promulgating what can only be termed 'fake news'. This issue is insightfully dissected in Eric Alterman's essay on think tanks.[40] Here the appropriate conclusion to draw is perhaps that the rise of fake news and of ideologically motivated think tanks really point up a responsibility on intellectuals not so much to 'lift the veil of ideology' as to teach people how to do this for themselves by showing them how to analyse and question the sources of news. As he says in the same paper, 'The basis of democracy is not information but conversation'.

A further corollary of these developments is that speaking truth is not enough: you need to take steps to ensure that others hear the truth and can disentangle it from the sea of disinformation flooding the web. What do intellectuals now have to do to get the truth across and ensure that the general public (or the educated general public, or whoever the intended audience is) have some exposure to it? Are new responsibilities emerging not just to speak truth but to do so in particular ways, such as through social media, or particular channels, such as WikiTribune?

Making the truth actionable

Quoting Daniel Bell's *The End of Ideology*, Chomsky talks in RoI of 'the conversion of ideas into social levers'.[41] If we take our responsibilities seriously we must talk sufficiently persuasively that those who hear us take action. As Nicholas Allott stresses in his contribution to this volume, this is not a simple thing to do. One problematic finding – the 'backfire' effect – is that facts that contradict political beliefs tend to reinforce rather than dispel those beliefs: we treat these facts with suspicion, while uncritically welcoming evidence that confirms our current view.[42] Shamefully, the same applies even in academe. A further problem is that action is frequently not driven by evaluation of the consequences, as witness voting behaviour, which is typically neither a matter of selecting a party with policies that match preferences nor of rewarding or punishing incumbents for their actions. Voting patterns are strongly affected by natural events: incumbents have been punished for bad weather and shark attacks.[43] So simply exposing facts is radically insufficient: we have at a minimum a responsibility to tell the truth in ways that make it likely to be grasped and acted upon. In a nutshell, intellectuals have a responsibility to ensure that the truth is accessible not just to other intellectuals but to the population at large.

In many areas where some progress is undeniable, economic class still impacts hugely upon the practical enjoyment of civil and political rights. The interest that western intellectuals have had in speaking truth to power has been greatest where it has influenced their own rights as opposed to those of an economic or political underclass. A simple but topical example is the systematic distortion of debate around UK housing policy, where many intellectuals are happy to bemoan the lack of supply, which directly disadvantages them, but fewer discuss the changes to the benefit system and the powers of local authorities which have disenfranchised the poor; still less how the situation could be improved.[44]

Even-handed exposure of the truth as it affects all in society may not be sufficient. With many issues (climate change, migration, inequality) it is probable that significant numbers of people know the truth – but are unwilling to make the sacrifices required to rectify the situation.[45] To what extent do intellectuals have a responsibility to come up with solutions that show people how they can do the right thing without making sacrifices they're just not prepared to make? Alternatively, to what extent do intellectuals have a responsibility to demonstrate by example that making the sacrifices is not as impossible as it seems and still leaves one with a worthwhile existence?

More challenging is how to determine what responsibilities intellectuals face when speaking truth to power is insufficient and one needs to change the *structures* of power. Consider the case of women's rights and the associated issue of women's power in society. If we restrict attention to western Europe and north America, there has clearly been considerable progress, but it is significant that we still need to talk about women 'breaking through the glass ceiling'. In a perceptive essay, Mary Beard observes that our 'cultural template for a powerful person remains resolutely male', talking of how this template 'works to disempower women' and noting that 'You can't easily fit women into a structure that is already coded as male; you have to change the structure'.[46] How far beyond merely pointing out these truths do an intellectual's responsibilities go?

As these examples make obvious, an element of activism is required over and above just *speaking* the truth, if that truth is to be actionable. Activism can take many forms, ranging from monumental linked movements exemplified by the 'Arab Spring' or 'Black Lives Matter'[47] to individual acts of raising awareness. Activism is often most powerful when it includes an element of demonstrating the art of the possible. It need not be focused on global issues to be valuable – innumerable issues are worth supporting and defending. To take one small example, consider Heineken's WOBO – the brewer's 'World Bottle'. On a visit to the Caribbean, the brewing magnate Alfred Heineken identified two problems: bottles littering the beaches and a serious lack of building materials. He proposed solving both problems by inventing a bottle that could function as a brick. Sadly, the idea was a 'failure' in that it never took off; but it is an example of what individuals can do – and arguably intellectuals must now do. In his *Requiem for the American Dream*, Chomsky emphasises that 'activists are the people who have created the rights that we enjoy', and ends the book with Howard Zinn's words 'what matters is the countless small deeds of unknown people, who lay the basis for the significant events that enter history'.[48]

Broader issues

In RoI, Chomsky focused on the responsibility of individual intellectuals to speak the truth and expose lies. But if they are to be able to do that in a way that has an impact, there are perhaps prior responsibilities that need exploring.

'Civic space' and the infringement of liberties

Above we touched on changes to the academic environment that may discourage at least one set of intellectuals from speaking out. But there are much broader changes at play as well. 'Civic space' is the set of conditions that enable citizens to organise, participate and communicate without hindrance. Civic space is only secure when a state protects its citizens and 'respects and facilitates their fundamental rights to associate, assemble peacefully and freely express views and opinions'.[49]

As the organisation Civicus demonstrates,[50] there is ample evidence that civic space is under attack around the world, and that vulnerable groups are discouraged from speaking out, often under the pretext that this is a necessary part of the counter-terrorism agenda. To take a simple example, as part of its attempt to stop 'radicalisation', the UK government instituted the 'Prevent' strategy.[51] Among other measures this provision requires that social services, faith leaders, teachers, doctors and others refer those at risk of radicalisation to a local Prevent body, which then decides what to do. Among the signs that someone may warrant referral is 'having a sense of grievance that is triggered by personal experience of racism or discrimination or aspects of government policy'.[52]

The *Civicus Monitor* goes on to point out how developments in the UK mirror more draconian actions elsewhere, making the obvious but helpful point that it is important for governments in the global north to practise what they preach if they are to have any credibility when criticising the actions of governments in the global south.

This suggests that there is a new responsibility on intellectuals: to defend the civic space that makes possible the exercise of the responsibilities outlined in RoI, and to show solidarity with those human rights defenders globally trying to do the same.

Liberty

The changes in the powers of the UK government touched on above reflect ideologically motivated infringement of liberties more generally. This can be illustrated with a motion brought at the 2017 annual general meeting of the civil liberties and human rights charity Liberty, attacking aspects of the UK government's regressive legislation:[53]

> This AGM condemns the use of discrimination and destitution as public policy tools to discourage migration. This AGM resolves to fight to dismantle this deeply unethical strategy including campaigning against:
>
>> The requirement on schools to collect nationality and country of birth data on children;
>>
>> Home Office agreements with the Department for Education and the NHS regarding data sharing for immigration purposes;
>>
>> The requirement on landlords to check tenants' rights to reside in the UK and associated penalties;
>>
>> The requirement on banks and healthcare providers to check residency rights;

The new criminal offences of 'driving while illegal' and 'working while illegal'; and … that no human being is 'illegal', such a concept is totally unacceptable.

The need for such a set of proposals is a harsh indictment of current ideology, where 'ideology' is described by Bell,[54] in terms that Chomsky endorses, as 'a mask for class interest'. The issue should serve as a rallying call for responsible intellectuals whose 'role in the creation and analysis of ideology' should be 'our basic concern'.[55]

Global domains

Individual intellectuals have a responsibility 'to speak the truth and to expose lies', and we have suggested above that they must undertake an element of activism if this is to have any impact. However, it is characteristic of many of the issues most critical for human survival (e.g. climate change) that they quite clearly need a global response, including from countries such as China that are not western democracies. While Chomsky's usual strictures about being responsible for the actions of one's own country and the emptiness of attacking the actions of other countries still apply, it remains true that genuine progress on these issues will require international collaboration. Intellectuals, especially those with international networks, such as most academics, plausibly have a responsibility to foster such collaboration and to ensure that the truth they speak is accessible not just locally but globally. Chomsky's own practice provides some clues as to what this might involve. He not only talks and writes fanatically hard (with a great deal of his work accessible on the internet), he has visited Turkey to support Fatih Tas; he went to Nicaragua to show solidarity with the Sandinistas; he went to North Vietnam to provide less biased reportage on the situation there;[56] the list is almost endless. He is a paradigmatic example of an intellectual who has confronted the emerging responsibility to do more to spread the word and support activism on a global scale. Supporting the networks that make global action possible is perhaps another new responsibility for the value-oriented intellectual.

Conclusion

By exploring some of the developments that have occurred over the last 50 years we have reinforced the conclusion that the responsibilities of intellectuals that Chomsky set out in his paper still have their original force. There have been subtle changes concerning the ways in which speaking the truth and exposing lies have got harder. But public awareness of the needs is also greater, leaving room for modest optimism.

When he wrote RoI, Chomsky recognised that the responsibilities he discussed were just the start. As he wrote in response to a letter from George Steiner:

> I do feel that the crucial question, unanswered in the article, is what the next paragraph should say. I've thought a good deal about this, without having reached any satisfying conclusions. I've tried various things – harassing congressmen, 'lobbying' in Washington, lecturing at town forums, working with student groups in preparation of public protests, demonstrations, teach-ins, and so on, in all of the ways that many others have adopted as well. The only respect in which I have personally gone any further is in refusal to pay half of my income tax … My own feeling is that one should refuse to participate in any activity that implements American aggression – thus tax refusal, draft refusal, avoidance of work that can be used by the agencies of militarism and repression, all seem to me essential. I can't suggest a general formula. Detailed decisions have to be matters of personal judgement and conscience. I feel uncomfortable about suggesting draft refusal publicly, since it is a rather cheap proposal from someone of my age. But I think that tax refusal is an important gesture, both because it symbolizes a refusal to make a voluntary contribution to the war machine and also because it indicates a willingness, which should, I think, be indicated, to take illegal measures to oppose an indecent government.[57]

Now, 50 years on, the need for all of us to examine our consciences and decide 'What have I done?' and 'What can I do?' has never been greater.

Notes

1 We are grateful to Nicholas Allott and two anonymous reviewers for perceptive comments on an earlier version.
2 Conor Friedersdorf, 'What James Clapper doesn't understand about Edward Snowden,' *The Atlantic*, 24 February 2014, https://www.theatlantic.com/politics/archive/2014/02/what-james-clapper-doesnt-understand-about-edward-snowden/284032/ (accessed February 2018).
3 Noam Chomsky, 'Chomsky on Snowden & why NSA surveillance doesn't stop terror while the U.S. drone war creates it,' interview by Amy Goodman, *Democracy Now*, 3 March 2015,

https://www.democracynow.org/2015/3/3/chomsky_on_snowden_why_nsa_surveillance (accessed September 2018).

4   See for example Dwight Macdonald, *The Responsibility of Peoples and Other Essays in Political Criticism* (London: Gollancz, 1957).

5   Noam Chomsky in *Language and Politics*, ed. Carlos P. Otero (Montréal: Black Rose Books, 1988), 173.

6   Noam Chomsky, 'The responsibility of intellectuals, redux: Using privilege to challenge the state,' *Boston Review*, 1 September 2011.

7   See Noam Chomsky, *Requiem for the American Dream: The Principles of Concentrated Wealth and Power* (New York: Seven Stories Press, 2017), 20 (Principle #2) for recent discussion.

8   According to Waseem Yaqoob in the *London Review of Books*, 'figures from 2016 showed that 75,000 UK university staff were on highly casualised contracts, and 21,000 on zero hours'. Waseem Yaqoob, 'Why we strike,' *London Review of Books*, 16 February 2018.

9   See Walker's contribution in Chapter 2. Of equal importance to ethnicity is the question of class. (For some relevant discussion see Owen Jones, *Chavs: The Demonization of the Working Class* (London: Verso, 2011).)

10 Alan Lightman, 'The role of the public intellectual: Remarks presented to the MIT Communications Forum "Public Intellectuals and the Academy",' 2 December 1999, http://www.mit.edu/~saleem/ivory/epil.htm

11 Cited in Chomsky, *Requiem for the American Dream* (2017), 123. Elsewhere, when Chomsky mentions Hume's paradox, he suggests that Hume may have been too sanguine about the power relations involved. See Neil Smith and Nicholas Allott, *Chomsky: Ideas and Ideals*, 3rd ed. (Cambridge: Cambridge University Press, 2016), 314–5.

12 For an analysis of Chomsky's own 'technique of dissection' see Smith and Allott, *Chomsky* (2016), 321 ff.

13 Sophie Chappell, 'Political deliberation under conditions of deception: The case of Brexit,' *Think* 15 (2016): 7–13.

14 The NRA describes itself, somewhat to our surprise, as 'the oldest continuously operating *civil rights* organization in the United States' (our emphasis). This claim was once generally accepted but is now treated with some scepticism: see https://en.wikipedia.org/wiki/National_Rifle_Association (accessed 4 November 2018). It is significant that the cause of the scepticism is that other civil rights organisations pre-dated the NRA.

15 For a number of examples, see *The Corporate Legal Accountability Quarterly Bulletin* (BHRRC, September 2017): 24.

16 The Business and Human Rights Resource Centre, https://www.business-humanrights.org/ (accessed February 2018).

17 Peter Beinart, 'Trump's anti-Muslim political strategy,' *The Atlantic*, 29 November 2017, https://www.theatlantic.com/politics/archive/2017/11/trumps-anti-muslim-retweets-shouldnt-surprise-you/547031/ (accessed July 2018).

18 Faiz Siddiqui, 'Uber triggers protest for not supporting taxi strike against refugee ban,' *Washington Post* (29 January 2017), https://www.washingtonpost.com/news/dr-gridlock/wp/2017/01/29/uber-triggers-protest-for-not-supporting-taxi-strike-against-refugee-ban/?utm_term=.0683616f04a5 (accessed February 2018). By way of contrast, downloads of the app for Uber's smaller rival Lyft (which donated US$1 million to the American Civil Liberties Union) surged and briefly surpassed downloads of the Uber app.

19 Eric March, 'USA CEO Of Penzeys Spices achieves sales surge by standing up against discriminatory rhetoric,' https://www.business-humanrights.org/en/usa-ceo-of-penzeys-spices-achieves-sales-surge-by-standing-up-against-discriminatory-rhetoric (accessed February 2018).

20 We are grateful to Mauricio Lazala, Gregory Regaignon and Marti Flacks of the Business and Human Rights Resource Centre for helpful discussion of these examples.

21 Noam Chomsky and Harry Belafonte, 'The search for the rebel heart,' Interview by Amy Goodman and Juan González, *Democracy Now*, 7 December 2016, https://www.democracynow.org/2016/12/7/the_search_for_the_rebel_heart (accessed November 2018). See also Chomsky *Optimism over Despair* (London: Penguin, 2017).

22 Noam Chomsky and David Barsamian, *Chronicles of Dissent* (Stirling: AK Press, 1992), 354.

23 Leo Benedictus, 'Noam Chomsky on Donald Trump: "Almost a death knell for the human species",' *The Guardian*, 20 May 2016.

24 The case against such questioning of the existence of objective truth is succinctly put in Smith and Allott, *Chomsky* (2016), 268: 'The claim that all argument is subjective can itself be subjected to critical (rational) analysis. If it is an objective claim it is contradictory: it would be false if true. If it is a subjective claim then, by hypothesis, it cannot exclude the objective claim that it is false. On either interpretation the thesis is self-defeating'.

25 Thomas Nagel, *The Last Word* (Oxford: Oxford University Press, 1997); Paul Boghossian, *Fear of Knowledge* (Oxford: Oxford University Press, 2007) (we are grateful to an anonymous reviewer for drawing this book to our attention); on the Chomsky/Foucault debate see Peter Wilkin, *Noam Chomsky: On Power, Knowledge and Human Nature* (London: Macmillan Press, 1997), 77 ff. Video and a transcript of the debate are easily found online.

26 Boghossian, *Fear of Knowledge*, 130.

27 On 'no platforming' or the 'free speech' debate, see for example Eric Heinze, 'Ten arguments for – and against – "no-platforming",' last modified 28 March 2016, http://freespeechdebate. com/discuss/ten-arguments-for-and-against-no-platforming/

28 Paul Krugman, 'The new political correctness,' *New York Times* blog post, 26 May 2012, https://krugman.blogs.nytimes.com/2012/05/26/the-new-political-correctness/ (accessed 28 May 2018).

29 Tom Nichols, *The Death of Expertise: The Campaign Against Established Knowledge and Why it Matters* (Oxford: Oxford University Press, 2016). There is a long history of anti-intellectualism on both sides of the political spectrum. On the right, it goes back at least to the counter-enlightenment (Berlin, 1973). Crudely, the wellspring seems always to have been that the ideas promoted by the 'intellectuals' would pose a challenge to traditional forms of authority and political organisation. Perhaps for this reason, the intellectuals who have most often been the target have been teachers and academics. This tradition plausibly lies behind some of the distrust of experts expressed by people like Michael Gove. If one looks at the political left, there is also a long history of anti-intellectual distrust of experts, though primarily from a feeling that the experts try to speak for the people, instead of letting them speak for themselves – inevitably getting it wrong in the process. As a result, the left-wing distrust of experts has been focused on 'political' experts. Arguably, the two traditions have now coalesced into a general distrust of experts, as amply illustrated by the examples in Nichols' *The Death of Expertise* (2016). One aspect of the recent rise of anti-intellectualism that hasn't received the attention it deserves is the possible link to a corporate agenda. As Chomsky has frequently emphasised, corporations benefit politically from a passive and disengaged populace (leaving corporate lobbyists free to pull the strings), and anything that rubbishes critical thought and the pronouncements of intellectuals is likely to find favour with them. The connections between anti-intellectualism and corporate think tanks merit further study.

30 Noam Chomsky, 'The responsibility of intellectuals,' in Noam Chomsky, *American Power and the New Mandarins* (1969), 125.

31 Nichols, *The Death of Expertise* (2016), 4.

32 Andrew Wakefield's debunked programme attributing the increased incidence of autism to the effect of the MMR vaccine is currently enjoying considerable success in Houston: see Jessica Glenza, 'Disgraced anti-vaxxer Andrew Wakefield aims to advance his agenda in Texas election,' *The Guardian*, 26 February 2018. https://www.theguardian.com/us-news/2018/ feb/26/texas-vaccinations-safety-andrew-wakefield-fear-elections (accessed 28 May 2018).

33 He cites Nichols, *The Death of Expertise* (2016), 209–10, the same quotation as we do below.

34 While many of the targets Nichols attacks deserve his condemnation, it is striking that his own scholarship is unreliable. Apart from the presumption that his own expertise is genuine and reliable, with a depth not accessible to the interested layman, he attacks Chomsky for his 'lack of credentials' and being 'no more an expert in foreign policy than, say, the late George Kennan was in the origins of human language' (44). Needless to say, there are no citations of any of Chomsky's 'stack of books on politics and foreign policy', not a single example of anything Chomsky having written or said being incorrect or misleading, nor any engagement with Chomsky's claim that pretensions of expertise in 'political science' are largely fraudulent.

35 In an interview on 6 June 2016 with Faisal Islam; reported by Chatham House, 'Michael Gove on the Trouble With Experts', 3 March 2017, https://www.chathamhouse.org/expert/ comment/michael-gove-trouble-experts (accessed 6 November 2018)

36 The convention in deaf studies is to use 'Deaf' for members of the Deaf community and 'deaf' to describe people who happen to be audiologically deaf. See for example Gary Morgan and

Bencie Woll, *Directions in Sign Language Acquisition* (Amsterdam: John Benjamins Publishing Co., 2002), xx. As approximately 90 per cent of deaf children are born to hearing parents and may have no exposure to usable language for months or years, many deaf people are not members of the Deaf community. Similarly, hearing people with deaf/Deaf parents can become part of the Deaf community.

37 Pamela B. Rutledge, 'Four ways social media is redefining activism,' *Psychology Today* (2010), https://www.psychologytoday.com/gb/blog/positively-media/201010/four-ways-social-media-is-redefining-activism (accessed 28 May 2018); Ryanne Lau, 'Social media as tool for meaningful political activism,' *McGill Left Review*, 9 March 2017, http://mcgillleftreview.com/article/social-media-tool-meaningful-political-activism (accessed 28 May 2018).

38 See for example Eytan Bakshy, Solomon Messing and Lada Adamic, 'Exposure to ideologically diverse news and opinion on Facebook,' *Science* 348, no. 6239 (2015): 1130–2.

39 Chomsky, *Requiem for the American Dream* (2017), 4.

40 Eric Alterman, 'The professors, the press, the think tanks – and their problems,' *Bulletin of the American Association of University Professors* (May–June 2011).

41 It should be emphasised that Chomsky was in radical disagreement with Bell's thesis of 'the end of ideology'. Daniel Bell, *The End of Ideology: On the Exhaustion of Political Ideas in the Fifties* (New York: The Free Press, 1962).

42 David McRaney, 'The backfire effect,' You Are Not So Smart website, 10 June 2011, https://youarenotsosmart.com/2011/06/10/the-backfire-effect/ (accessed February 2018).

43 Debra Liese, 'What do sharks have to do with democracy? Christopher Achen and Larry Bartels explain,' Princeton University Press blog, 31 March 2016, http://blog.press.princeton.edu/2016/03/31/what-do-sharks-have-to-do-with-democracy-christopher-achen-larry-bartels-explain/ (accessed February 2018).

44 See Anna Minton, *Big Capital: Who is London For?* (London: Penguin, 2017).

45 For a sustained meditation on inequality, see Chomsky, *Requiem for the American Dream* (2017), 148.

46 Mary Beard, 'Women in power,' *London Review of Books* 39, no. 6 (2017).

47 Founded by three women – Patrice Cullors, Alicia Garza and Opal Tometi – whose names are not usually reported.

48 Chomsky, *Requiem for the American Dream* (2017), 148.

49 Civicus, 'CIVICUS Monitor: Tracking Civic Space,' http://www.civicus.org/index.php/what-we-do/knowledge-analysis/civicus-monitor (accessed February 2018).

50 'A global alliance of civil society organisations and activists dedicated to strengthening citizen action and civil society throughout the world.' Civicus, 'Who we are,' https://www.civicus.org/index.php/who-we-are/about-civicus (accessed 28 May 2018).

51 BBC, 'Reality Check: What is the Prevent strategy?' *BBC News*, 4 June 2017, http://www.bbc.co.uk/news/election-2017-40151991 (accessed February 2018); Prevent is one part of 'Contest', the other parts being 'Prepare, Protect, and Pursue'.

52 See Karma Nabulsi, 'Don't go to the Doctor,' *London Review of Books* 39, no. 10 (2016): 27–8. It is perhaps hardly surprising that many individuals and organisations, most notably the Muslim Council of Britain and the National Union of Students, perceive Prevent as counter-productive or even 'toxic', as it can make Islamic students, for example, feel isolated, unwelcome and unsafe – and possibly more open to radicalisation. Miqdaad Versi, 'Prevent is failing. Any effective strategy must include Muslim communities,' *The Guardian*, 20 October 2016, https://www.theguardian.com/commentisfree/2016/oct/20/prevent-isnt-working-inclusive-muslim-communities-counter-terrorism (accessed 4 November 2018).

53 Liberty, https://www.liberty-human-rights.org.uk/ (accessed February 2018). The 2017 AGM can be found at https://www.libertyhumanrights.org.uk/sites/default/files/Resolutions%20of%20the%20AGM%202017.pdf (accessed 4 November 2018).

54 Bell, *The End of Ideology* (1962).

55 Noam Chomsky, 'The responsibility of intellectuals,' in Noam Chomsky, *American Power and the New Mandarins* (New York: Vintage Books, 1969), 343.

56 Noam Chomsky, 'In North Vietnam,' *New York Review of Books*, 13 August 1970.

57 Noam Chomsky, '"The Responsibility of Intellectuals": An exchange,' *New York Review of Books*, 23 March 1967.

2

'I don't want no peace' – a black, Jewish activist's take on the responsibility of intellectuals

Jackie Walker

> I don't want no peace,
> I need equal rights and justice.
> – Peter Tosh, *Equal Rights and Justice*

> The ideas of the ruling class are in every epoch the ruling ideas.
> – Karl Marx, *The German Ideology*

Genocide

Professor Chomsky's 1967 essay, 'The Responsibility of Intellectuals', was written in the context of the ongoing American invasion of Vietnam. American post-Second World War optimism was fading as stories of defeat and American savagery and scenes of GIs on the rampage overlapped with homegrown footage of white barbarity waged against black fellow citizens. Some consider this a turning point in American consciousness.

For people of colour, forever excluded from the dream of America, this 'fall from grace' was no turning point. It was simply another encounter with the truth as they lived it, as victims, with the native peoples of America, of what Chomsky describes as 'one of the two founding crimes of American society', an America built on genocide, enslavement and oppression.[1]

What is due to Caesar?

Today, while Donald Trump's election campaign suggested a desire for decreased US involvement overseas, his presidential rhetoric implies a resurgence of crude nationalism. It suggests an America unwilling to accept limitations to its power, with calls for a fight to the finish with ISIS, assurances of increased support for Israel and an escalation of its nuclear arsenals. While this time round the bogey-man is terrorist Muslims rather than Communists, there's a whiff of Senator McCarthy to Trumpism, an authoritarian politics backed by a good helping of the witch-hunt, fake news, smears and scapegoating.

Why worry, some say. After all, America is two thousand miles away and has long been our ally. What's changed? Well, plenty is the answer. As the UK moves towards an unknown post-Brexit situation, pressure to get closer to Uncle Sam will increase, whoever its president is, however crazed he may seem. Attacks on minorities are increasing and Chomsky's assertion that intellectuals have a responsibility to speak truth feels ever more like a clarion call, whatever the colour of our skin.

Intellectuals, those who have the ability to reflect, comment and propose solutions on what they see, are not however a homogenous group, and it takes more than intelligence to see beyond the prevailing ideas of the ruling class in order, as Edward Said said, to 'present alternative narratives and other perspectives'.[2] And the truth is that many intellectuals promote, or turn a blind eye, to the oppressions of the establishment. Financial inducements increase this complicity.

The establishment's control over university academics, along with other public servants and institutions, has if anything increased over recent years due to the pressures of cuts and job insecurity. All these are problematic, but I'm not concerned here with the 'lackeys of the establishment' whatever form they take. I'm interested in intellectuals who see their role as more than just suggesting solutions. It is to those people these remarks are addressed.

How far is it to the bottom?

The global economic crash, the long-term crisis of capitalism, has resulted in the rise of demagogic leaders. The forces of the right, aided by the mainstream media, first undermined the vocabulary of liberation as 'political correctness' and then appropriated our hard-fought-for formulations of identity, our histories of oppression, in order to enhance their reactionary narratives. We see this for example in an increasing tendency to normalise constructions of whites as a group under siege. Of course this crude populism, a reaching out to the 'common man' – very rarely the 'common woman' – reinforces the power of the establishment that these demagogues claim to challenge.

In Britain the left is now under sustained attack as a consequence of its success in knocking at the doors of power. It is no coincidence that among the tools used to undermine, fracture and attempt to defeat us is the appropriated language of liberation – in particular that of race. Since Jeremy Corbyn became leader of the Labour Party we've seen the most sustained attention on racism I've ever known, in an ongoing debate focused on antisemitism.

Of course, all racism, whether Islamophobia, antisemitism or any other type, is abhorrent. But the palatable nature of critiquing a racism decoupled from notions of power, or the lack of it, has proved a powerful tool with which the establishment can attack the left – and they have run with it. False allegations of antisemitism have proliferated. This whitewashed version of anti-racism is one wherein racists are not Tory ministers who ridicule the appearance of people of African descent, and it certainly isn't those complaining about a Muslim woman reporter wearing a headscarf. Conveniently it's the left who are the culprits in this new racism. And on the left, it's our very commitment to anti-racism that is used against us, to undermine the unity we need so badly in order to resist this particular onslaught – as well, of course, as an inability to get reasonable access to the mainstream media, however much we have tried.

It is not a coincidence that the most oppressed minorities have barely registered in this dialogue – except as the accused; at best they have been called ignorant where racism is concerned. Black voices have yet again been effectively silenced, this time under a wave of self-righteous indignation voiced by some of the most reactionary forces in and outside the media. This new anti-racism simply has the effect of continuing the oppression of minorities with which it pretends concern. The exclusion of working-class people, the exclusion of the left from power, by all means that can be mustered, adds to a growing sense of the divisions between 'us' and 'them'. The very few of 'us' who get any influence are speedily and easily incorporated or destroyed.

Who are the criminals?

We inhabit a world where politics increasingly appears like a fraud perpetrated by interest groups, backed by the power of an economic and political elite who control what is said and what you can say, and who disseminate what they choose in order to keep control of what they increasingly have. This is the world as I have long lived it. For the truth is, while I do have a Jewish heritage, it is, in particular, my black voice that speaks in this essay, and as a black woman I inhabit a markedly different set of realities to fellow contributors to this collection of essays.

Fundamentally divorced from the structures of power, carrying the stigma of historical oppression on my skin, for me as a black woman even the concept of 'the intellectual' needs fundamental rethinking if it is not to be practically meaningless, simply another tool to exclude me. No post-war uplift has raised blacks from ghetto to power. Historical injustices against blacks remain barely acknowledged, let alone commemorated; it is with trepidation that people of colour lift their heads to speak truth to power on any issue, even those that relate to their own history and experience, for fear they find themselves derided at best, the subject of witch-hunts or threats of violence at the worst.

At this point, I should point out that in 2015 I became vice-chair of Momentum, the left-wing movement in the British Labour Party. Like Chomsky, I have been accused of antisemitism due both to my criticisms of Israeli policies and to perspectives I have voiced on some aspects of Jewish history – comments which have been quoted out of context and distorted for cynical reasons by the pro-Israel lobby and by opponents of Jeremy Corbyn's leadership of the British Labour Party. In September 2016, a media campaign around my supposed antisemitism led to my provisional suspension from the Labour Party. Chomsky is one of several Jewish intellectuals to have lent public support to my campaign to be reinstated.

I am told, by people who should know, that the campaign against me – not just the online abuse, but the well-orchestrated attempts to have me excluded from speaking at meetings, to exclude me from political activity – is something people have not seen in Britain before. For to tell the truth, to disturb the 'intentional ignorance' of Euro-American society, is to infringe a taboo that is savagely policed and maintained.

Of course there are, and have been, individual black voices that have gained attention, but in Britain, black academics lack the numbers to be significant. The best universities and schools remain mostly closed to us. Except in popular culture, sport, prisons and arriving too early at the graveyard, people of colour continue to be excluded at all levels, including from left-wing politics, where too often we are used as tokens to decorate some faux liberal agenda, or moved like pawns to further other people's careers, where we are repeatedly asked – or, in my most recent experience, 'told' – to stay silent: 'let's just get power first and we'll deal with *you* next'. Or even worse: 'We know you're right, but if we do anything, the media will rip us to shreds.'

Yet if it is our duty to speak truth to power, as black and oppressed peoples, as people who seek the liberation of humanity, those of us who heed that call *must* act on it, in whatever way we are able – and, let's be clear, the cost can be high; it can be everything.

Give it up

It was this call that joined my black mother of Jewish descent and my Russian Jewish father – she a political activist, he a Communist – to attempt revolution and resistance against 1950s American culture. They risked their lives, were tortured, derided and disposed of. Their people were black and white, Jew and Gentile. Their concerns encompassed the liberation of humankind. And so, as my mothers and fathers did before me, I fight for emancipation, refuting ideologies that put one people's suffering, one people's claim to nationhood, above any other, rejecting boundaries that separate, refusing to move to the back of the bus, to play the minstrel, to remain dumb and blinded because the media, or anyone else, says I should do so.

'I don't want no peace, I want equal rights and justice.' This is the demand Peter Tosh speaks, or rather sings. He dances as he lays his challenge at the door of an establishment that presents itself as valorising peace and quietude while simultaneously enforcing a violent and destructive status quo. Tosh's speech is directed to the mass of the people, his ideas formulated in a genre that can be heard by any who choose to hear and take up its rhythms.

A development of Tosh's words, 'No justice, no peace', has become the marching cry of black activists and protestors on both sides of the Atlantic. These are the intellectuals of our movement, the mothers and fathers, cooks and cleaners, the unemployed, fast-food workers, the office workers – all are our intellectuals, all who resist while standing witness to the truth.

Chomsky's essay, the subject of this book, was a response to an earlier work, 'The Responsibility of Peoples', a collection of essays written by Dwight Macdonald. What is the responsibility of any intellectual if it is not wedded to the interests of the people? And while separation from power is a particular and acute problem for black intellectuals, it is a problem shared by all intellectuals, all people who seek global transformations.

To take on the responsibility of the intellectual is to be part of a movement for change, discarding the trappings that separate thought from action, body from mind, that confine some of us to action in the classroom and others to the streets. Until the streets become the classrooms and the classrooms the streets our task as intellectuals will be incomplete. It is a necessary journey. It will be a long and perilous one.

Notes

1   Noam Chomsky and George Yancy, 'Noam Chomsky on the roots of American racism,' *New York Times*, 18 March 2018, https://opinionator.blogs.nytimes.com/2015/03/18/noam-chomsky-on-the-roots-of-american-racism/ (accessed February 2018).
2   Edward Said, *Humanism and Democratic Criticism* (New York: Columbia University Press, 2004), 141.

3

The responsibility of intellectuals in the era of bounded rationality and *Democracy for Realists*

Nicholas Allott

In his famous essay, Chomsky wrote: 'It is the responsibility of intellectuals to speak the truth and to expose lies. This, at least, may seem enough of a truism to pass over without comment.'[1] One might ask what the source of this responsibility (henceforth RI) is. Chomsky notes that in western democracies, where there is 'political liberty, ... access to information and freedom of expression' a 'privileged minority' (whom he refers to as 'intellectuals') also have

> the leisure, the facilities, and the training to seek the truth lying hidden behind the veil of distortion and misrepresentation, ideology and class interest, through which the events of current history are presented to us.[2]

They therefore have responsibilities that go beyond those of others.

Agreeing with this, one might note that RI seems to presuppose that exposing political truths has a certain kind of instrumental value, namely that it will tend to make the world a better place by changing people's political views.[3] In fact, Chomsky's position on this question is more nuanced. In an interview he said 'I don't have faith that the truth will prevail if it becomes known, but we have no alternative to proceeding on that assumption', and he has often endorsed Gramsci's 'optimism of the will' as a necessary corollary to pessimism of the intellect.[4]

I suggest that intellectuals and other privileged individuals have the responsibility not only to tell the truth and expose lies but to do so in ways that – in their best judgement – are most likely to be understood and to be effective. This is a fairly direct consequence of another claim that Chomsky has made many times: that people are responsible for the foreseeable consequences of their actions. He calls this a truism, too, with some justification.

But why does the issue of effectiveness even arise? Isn't it enough simply to get the truth out in some form or other? Perhaps no one has ever held such a naive view; in any case, recent findings in psychology and political science make the challenges it faces more obvious and specific. They suggest that the truth does not necessarily influence political behaviour even when it is available, and that exposure to the truth may entrench rather than overthrow erroneous opinions.

There is strong evidence that voting is not driven primarily by evaluation of the policies on offer. Recently, the political scientists Christopher Achen and Larry Bartels have argued that voting is not well explained as selection of a party with policies that match the voter's preferences, nor as rewarding or punishing incumbents for their actions.[5] Evidence includes the startling fact that votes are strongly affected by natural events. If Achen and Bartels are right, then there is a significant disconnection between widely available information and one of the central ways that citizens exert political power, and it is natural to suppose that the story is similar for other political behaviour besides voting. The challenge to RI from this research is that telling the truth and exposing lies may not make much difference.

A second problem is indicated by research on motivated reasoning and the 'backfire effect'. Facts that contradict political beliefs or discredit voters' preferred electoral candidates tend to reinforce rather than dispel those beliefs and allegiances.[6] We have a strong tendency to treat such facts with suspicion, while uncritically welcoming evidence that confirms our current views. Clearly, the challenge to RI posed by this work is that telling the truth may be counterproductive and damaging.

In what follows, I first set out these research findings in a bit more detail, then consider how troubling these results – if real and robust – are for RI. In my discussion, I briefly show that Achen and Bartels' results are highly congruent with Chomsky's views on the functioning of education systems, the mass media and representative democracy in the US and other modern democracies. It is plausible that deepening democracy so that it more closely matches the popular ideal will require considerable changes to education, the media and the democratic system itself.

If the backfire effect is dominant then RI will often be overridden by a responsibility to avoid harm. But the findings about the backfire effect need to be weighed up against other evidence that telling the truth can change opinions in positive ways.

The problematic findings

Democracy for Realists

In their recent book, Achen and Bartels claim that there is a dominant folk theory or popular ideal of democracy,[7] which can be summarised in this way:

> Ordinary people have preferences about what their government should do. They choose leaders who will do those things, or they enact their preferences directly in referendums. In either case, what the majority wants becomes government policy.[8]

Summarising a great deal of evidence, they argue that this theory is wrong:

> The populist ideal of electoral democracy, for all its elegance and attractiveness, is largely irrelevant in practice, leaving elected officials mostly free to pursue their own notions of the public good or to respond to party and interest group pressures.[9]

A wealth of evidence suggests that votes are not cast on the basis of voters' policy preferences, and unsurprisingly, therefore, there is often a poor match between those preferences and the policies of the parties voted for.[10]

Achen and Bartels also argue that electoral choices do not support the retrospective voting hypothesis: that voters assess the performance of elected representatives and officials and punish or reward them accordingly at subsequent elections. They identify two reasons. First, voters are not good at distinguishing the effects caused by government policies from other effects. Achen and Bartels demonstrate this by showing that voters punish politicians for outcomes that are clearly not under their control, including natural events such as shark attacks, droughts and floods. Second, voters are not very good at keeping track of changes, even those that impact upon their own welfare. Achen and Bartels show that while voters do vote on the basis of income growth, there is a recency bias: we tend to focus on income growth in the months immediately prior to the election, neglecting the overall record of the government.

They also argue that so-called 'direct democracy', where voters vote on issues rather than for representatives, does not brighten the picture, because there is evidence that the results of such referendums and ballot initiatives reflect campaign spending by the wealthy more than the preferences of voters. In practice, Achen and Bartels argue – agreeing with work by David Broder – that the result of increased use of direct votes on issues, in the US at least, has largely been to empower the wealthy and well-organised 'millionaires and interest groups that use their wealth to achieve their own policy goals'.[11]

The true picture, Achen and Bartels argue, is that most voters pay little attention to politics, and at elections their choices depend largely on recent developments in the economy and on political group loyalties that are typically held from childhood.[12]

The backfire effect

A number of studies have found that evidence against a political or social belief may serve to strengthen that belief, and that negative information about a political candidate may increase the support she receives from those who already support her. Although these findings are striking, they should perhaps not be very surprising, given that there is a wealth of evidence from work over several decades in psychology and economics that human reasoning is prone to a wide variety of biases. We are very far from dispassionate, logical reasoners: our reasoning is often *motivated*, that is, slanted by our preconceptions and towards conclusions that we would prefer to be true, and much of it is performed by efficient but flawed heuristics rather than processes that respect laws of logic and statistical inference. What is more, we are not very reliable reporters of the way we reason. Introspection – that is, thinking about how one thinks – is not in general an accurate source of information.[13] The work discussed in this section extends this picture to political science.

Psychologists Kari Edwards and Edward Smith have shown a disconfirmation bias in reasoning about political and social issues: people examine arguments for longer on average if they clash with a belief that they hold, and a consequence of this longer examination is that such arguments are judged weaker on average than those that are compatible with prior beliefs. They also showed that this bias is greater when the belief that clashes with the argument is held with emotional conviction.[14] In a series of papers, political scientists Milton Lodge and Charles Taber find similar effects in our processing of information relating to issues such as gun control and affirmative action. The typical reaction to an argument against a prior belief or commitment is to generate counterarguments, whereas arguments that support prior beliefs are accepted uncritically.[15]

This tendency to generate counterarguments has a strikingly counterintuitive result: negative information can lead to a strengthening, rather than a weakening, of the initial belief.[16] This is the 'backfire effect', a term coined by Brendan Nyhan and Jason Reifler.[17] In their study, corrections of erroneous beliefs (e.g. that Iraq possessed weapons of mass destruction immediately before the US–UK invasion of 2003) led to reinforcement of the false belief.

Similar results emerge from work on (simulated) choice of political candidates. A study conducted by David Redlawsk found that voters took longer to process information that showed in a bad light a candidate whom the voter had already evaluated positively and information that showed in a good light a candidate already evaluated negatively, compared with information that fitted their expectations.[18] The backfire effect exists here too: negative information about a positively evaluated candidate tended to make that candidate *more* positively evaluated, not less.

In a later paper, Redlawsk and his co-authors Andrew Civettini and Karen Emmerson suggest an explanation:

> voters committed to a candidate may be motivated to discount incongruent information; they may mentally argue against it, bolstering their existing evaluation by recalling all the good things about a liked candidate even in the face of something negative.[19]

Taken together, this research suggests that we are very far from ideally rational, disinterested observers of the scene, updating our beliefs as warranted by new evidence. Under certain circumstances, we employ reasoning as a defence mechanism to bolster our prior convictions and choices against inconvenient truths.[20]

Discussion

How worried should a supporter of the responsibility of intellectuals be?

The *Democracy for Realists* findings are disturbing, but perhaps not as surprising for those on the left as they have been for some liberals and political scientists, since left-wingers of various persuasions have long argued that many people vote against their own interests (back at least to Engels' invocation of 'false consciousness').[21] In addition, Achen and

Bartels do not fully specify the mechanisms behind the effects they have discovered, leaving scope for supporters of RI to argue that part of the problem is that important truths are insufficiently well known and that lies go unchallenged. In that case, truth-telling by intellectuals could make a difference to how people vote. What is more, political change does not come about only, or even mainly, through choices at elections, and supporters of RI can argue that the responsibility to tell the truth is partly due to the effect a better-informed public may have in other ways, such as by improving the political culture.

The clash between the backfire effect and RI is harder to set aside. Revealing the truth about an issue, political party or candidate may have the opposite result to the one intended, entrenching opinions rather than changing them. To the extent that RI is motivated or justified by the expectation that exposing political truths will cause positive change, this is a fundamental challenge to the view. Happily, although the backfire effect is robust, there is convergent evidence that information can affect political views in non-perverse ways.

Bounded rationality

Both sets of findings have been connected with the fact that human rationality is bounded in various ways: by time, attention span, processing power and the competing demands of life.[22] We are finite beings, with only limited time and resources, and many other things to do besides keeping abreast of the activities of our governments; so, as Achen and Bartels write,

> In the welter of political claims and counterclaims, most people simply lack the time and relevant experience to sort out difficult truths from appealing dreams. That is no less true for Ivy League and Oxbridge dons than it is for average citizens.[23]

Given that Achen and Bartels' work does not specify in great detail the mechanisms that are responsible for their results,[24] a proponent of RI could argue that part of the problem is that those who could speak out do not do so, and this increases the amounts of time and attention required to get at the truth by sifting through the lies and evasions of politicians, columnists and the like. As Chomsky noted in his essay:

> The facts [about the US assault on Vietnam] are known to all who care to know. The press, foreign and domestic, has presented

documentation to refute each falsehood as it appears. But the power of the government's propaganda apparatus is such that the citizen who does not undertake a research project on the subject can hardly hope to confront government pronouncements with fact.

This is work that those with research skills and free time can usefully do, thus lowering the barriers somewhat for those who do not, although they are left, unavoidably, with the second-order research projects of deciding what to read and whether to believe it. Finding out about and critically reading the work of (e.g.) Patrick Cockburn and Tanya Reinhart on western Asia or Dean Baker and Ha-Joon Chang on economics takes considerable time and effort, but doing the work for oneself would take several lifetimes.[25]

The role of the media

Most adults get most of their information about politics and current affairs through the mass media. Obviously relevant, therefore, is Chomsky's work with Edward Herman on the ways that, in the formally free mass media in democratic societies, inconvenient facts are downplayed and debate is bounded by certain presuppositions that are neither questioned nor stated.[26] This work is highly congruent with Achen and Bartels' work; indeed it can be seen as suggesting mechanisms that help to cause the results they see:

> By manufacturing consent, you can overcome the fact that formally a lot of people have the right to vote. We can make it irrelevant because we can manufacture consent and make sure that their choices and attitudes will be structured in such a way that they will always do what we tell them, even if they have a formal way to participate.[27]

Assuming this is correct, the impact on RI is not obvious. Knowing that certain truths are off limits for the mass media arguably makes it more imperative for those who can to speak out. But this responsibility comes with a heavy dose of realism about getting views that are outside of the mainstream heard and understood.

The role of a good education

There are a number of other similarities between the views of Chomsky and Achen and Bartels. Chomsky has frequently made the claim that among the most thoroughly indoctrinated in modern democracies are the 'well-educated', that is, those who have spent longer than average in formal education, especially those who have attended elite institutions:

> If you've gone to the best schools … you just have instilled into you the understanding that there are certain things that [it] wouldn't do to say [a]nd, it wouldn't even do to think.[28]

In a similar vein, Achen and Bartels write that:

> Well-informed citizens['] … well-organized 'ideological' thinking often turns out to be just a rather mechanical reflection of what their favorite group and party leaders have instructed them to think.[29]

Obviously the picture is complicated by the fact that elite education is also conducive to the possession of skills that are needed for independent research and to the leisure required to put them to use, as Chomsky pointed out in 'The Responsibility of Intellectuals'.

The role of the democratic system

We've seen that Chomsky suggests that the media and the education system structure our attitudes. This could explain some part of Achen and Bartels' results. But, as discussed above, those results also show that people vote against their own preferences. Their explanation is that voting behaviour is better explained by the social group or groups to which a voter belongs.[30]

Another mechanism that very plausibly explains some of the mismatches between voter preferences and policy choices is the role of campaign finance. Thomas Ferguson's investment theory of party competition, often cited by Chomsky, postulates that the need to raise campaign finance ('the campaign cost condition') reduces party politics to 'competition between blocs of major investors'.[31] This means that voters are offered a choice between organisations that represent and will implement the preferred policies of certain areas of business, none of which is likely to match closely the preferences of ordinary voters. As Chomsky has pointed out, for a long time universal healthcare was the preference of the majority of voters in the US, but neither major party offered it.

It would seem that if one takes democracy seriously, one should work towards a system that is resilient against such distortions. Chomsky's vision here is of a bottom-up, citizen-led democracy:

> In a democratic system, what would happen [in the New Hampshire primary] is that the people in New Hampshire would get together in whatever organizations they have: town meetings, churches, unions, and work out what they want policy to be. Then, if some candidate wants to appeal to them, he could ask to be invited, and they would invite him to New Hampshire and tell him what they want. And, if they could get a commitment from him that they could believe in, they might decide to vote for him. That would be a democratic society.[32]

Assuming that Achen and Bartels are right, even if important truths become widely known in currently existing democracies, it is entirely possible that there will be little effect on how people vote. That is certainly chastening for supporters of RI, but in itself it is not enough to remove the responsibility, since it does not prove that telling the truth will not have an impact within the present system, and it shows little or nothing about whether it will aid in moving towards a more democratic society.

The backfire effect redux

If the backfire effect were always operative and dominant, then a key motivation for telling the truth and exposing lies would disappear, since telling the truth would generally be counterproductive.[33] But a moment's thought establishes that this cannot be right. People do change their minds, and at least some of the time when they do so it is because they have been persuaded by evidence against their prior belief.

In experimental work investigating the backfire effect, Redlawsk, Civettini and Emmerson found that there is a 'tipping point' beyond which further negative evidence has a negative effect rather than a reinforcing one.[34] As they say, this indicates that 'voters are not immune to disconfirming information after all, even when initially acting as motivated reasoners'.[35]

Other research shows that exposure to modest amounts of information can shift opinions considerably and that it has some effect on policy preferences. One strand of this research has focused on attitudes to immigration. In western countries, most people significantly overestimate the number of immigrants in their country, hold other inaccurate opinions about immigrants and would like immigration reduced. A large study carried out across 13 countries found that telling participants the correct percentage of immigrants in their country made it less likely that they would say that there are too many. In two studies in which participants were told five pieces of information about immigrants, this improved their attitudes toward immigrants. This information did not significantly change policy preferences on average, but it did make self-identified right-wingers and Republicans more likely to support pro-immigration policies, the opposite to what one might expect if the backfire effect were operative.[36] Similarly, a recent study carried out by Giovanni Facchini, Yotam Margalit and Hiroyuki Nakata in Japan – a country with very few immigrants and broad political opposition to immigration – found that hostility to increased immigration was considerably decreased by the presentation of information about potential social and economic benefits.[37]

It is clear, therefore, that it can be effective to expose people to information that tends to undermine their beliefs. Obviously, it would be useful to know more about when telling the truth is effective and when it is counterproductive. It is very plausible that the way that information is presented matters, in ways that we still know too little about. The research mentioned above on heuristics and biases is obviously relevant. It may also matter whether information is openly stated, implied or somehow presupposed. Such questions are the province of pragmatics, the area of linguistics that studies how we communicate with each other in context.[38] There is also a growing literature on the role of the salience of social group membership in receptiveness to information and argumentation.[39] As Alana Conner puts it: 'One of the things we know from social psychology is when people feel threatened, they can't change, they can't listen.'[40] In any case, the responsibility to tell the truth and expose lies remains, and is accompanied by a responsibility to do so effectively, which implies a further responsibility to keep abreast of research of the type discussed here as it develops.

Notes

1   Noam Chomsky, *American Power and the New Mandarins* (New York: New Press, 2002), 325.
2   Noam Chomsky, *American Power and the New Mandarins* (New York: New Press, 2002), 324.
3   Of course, telling the truth may be the right thing for intellectuals and others to do for other reasons, for example a Kantian or Christian prohibition on lies, or various possible instrumental roles of truth-telling other than informing people's first-order political behaviour

(e.g. it might promote trust in experts, and that might be a good). I proceed on the assumption that for Chomsky the effect of truth-telling on people's political views and therefore behaviour is a central reason for RI.

4   Noam Chomsky in *The Chomsky Reader*, ed. James Peck (London: Serpent's Tail, 1988), 48; Noam Chomsky and David Barsamian, *Secrets, Lies, and Democracy* (Tucson, AZ: Odonian Press, 1994), 354.

5   Christopher Achen and Larry Bartels, 'Democracy for realists: Holding up a mirror to the electorate,' *Juncture* 22, no. 4 (2016): 269–75; Christopher Achen and Larry Bartels, *Democracy for Realists: Why Elections Do Not Produce Responsive Government* (Princeton: Princeton University Press, 2016).

6   Milton Lodge and Charles S. Taber, 'Three steps toward a theory of motivated political reasoning,' in *Elements of Reason: Cognition, Choice, and the Bounds of Rationality*, eds Arthur Lupia, Matthew McCubbins and Samuel Popkin (Cambridge: Cambridge University Press, 2000); David P. Redlawsk, 'Hot cognition or cool consideration? Testing the effects of motivated reasoning on political decision making,' *The Journal of Politics* 64, no. 4 (2002); Brendan Nyhan and Jason Reifler, 'When corrections fail: The persistence of political misperceptions,' *Political Behavior* 32, no. 2 (2010).

7   As they discuss, there is a good deal of evidence that this folk theory co-exists with a realistic assessment of how things stand. In US polling a majority consistently agrees that 'the government is pretty much run by a few big interests looking out for themselves'. Achen and Bartels, *Democracy for Realists*, 8. See American National Election Studies Guide to Public Opinion, 'Is the government run for the benefit of all 1964–2012: Response "few big interests",' http://www.electionstudies.org/nesguide/graphs/g5a_2_1.htm (accessed February 2018).

8   Achen and Bartels, *Democracy for Realists*, 1.

9   Achen and Bartels, *Democracy for Realists*, 14.

10   Achen and Bartels, 'Democracy for realists,' 270.

11   David S. Broder, *Democracy Derailed: Initiative Campaigns and the Power of Money*, 1st ed. (New York: Harcourt, 2000), 1. This has been controversial in political science. Direct democracy in Switzerland seems to come closer to the popular ideal than in the US. Maduz (2010) is a useful review which tends to more positive conclusions about direct democracy. A recent paper by Prato and Strulovici (2017) provides a novel argument for a negative view. Linda Maduz, 'Direct democracy,' *Living Reviews in Democracy* 2 (2010); Carlo Prato and Bruno Strulovici, 'The hidden cost of direct democracy: How ballot initiatives affect politicians' selection and incentives,' *Journal of Theoretical Politics* 29, no. 3 (2017), 440–66.

12   Achen and Bartels, *Democracy for Realists*, 1. I do not attempt to evaluate Achen and Bartels' research here. My concern is with the consequences of their thesis, on the assumption that it is broadly correct, for RI. One scholarly response is that the findings are less surprising than Achen and Bartels suggest ('not news') and that their major contribution is 'interesting new data': Gerald Wright, 'A discussion of Christopher H. Achen and Larry M. Bartels' *Democracy for Realists: Why Elections Do Not Produce Responsive Government*,' *Perspectives on Politics* 15, no. 1 (2017), 161–2. For more positive assessments of its originality and impact see arguments by Neil Roberts, Andrew Sabl, Isabela Mares and Antje Schwennicke cited in 'A discussion of Christopher H. Achen and Larry M. Bartels' *Democracy for Realists*,' *Perspectives on Politics*, 148–61.

13   Daniel Kahneman and Amos Tversky, 'On the psychology of prediction,' *Psychological Review* 80, no. 4 (1973), is a classic early study on human irrationality; Daniel Kahneman, *Thinking, Fast and Slow* (New York: Farrar, Straus and Giroux, 2011) is a recent popular overview of the field. A classic study on the unreliability of introspection is Richard Nisbett and Timothy Wilson, 'Telling more than we can know: Verbal reports on mental processes,' *Psychological Review* 84, no. 3 (1977), 231. For a more optimistic take on heuristics in human reasoning and decision-making, see Gerd Gigerenzer, 'Why heuristics work,' *Perspectives on Psychological Science* 3, no. 1 (2008), 20–9.

14   Kari Edwards and Edward Smith, 'A disconfirmation bias in the evaluation of arguments,' *Journal of Personality and Social Psychology* 71, no. 1 (1996), 5–24.

15   E.g. Charles S. Taber and Milton Lodge, 'Motivated skepticism in the evaluation of political beliefs,' *American Journal of Political Science* 3, no. 50 (2006), 755–69.

16   Lodge and Taber, 'Three steps toward a theory of motivated political reasoning,' 183–213.

17 Brendan Nyhan and Jason Reifler, 'When corrections fail: The persistence of political misperceptions,' *Political Behavior* 32, no. 2 (2010), 303–30.

18 Redlawsk, 'Hot cognition or cool consideration?' *The Journal of Politics*: 1021–44.

19 David P. Redlawsk, Andrew J.W. Civettini and Karen M. Emmerson, 'The affective tipping point: Do motivated reasoners ever "get it"?' *Political Psychology* 31, no. 4 (2010), 567.

20 These findings are congruent with (although logically independent from) Mercier and Sperber's claim that the evolutionary function of the ability to reason is not to improve knowledge and make better decisions, but to help us to persuade others and to protect us against persuasion. However, to the extent that the results are problematic for RI, that is so regardless of any evolutionary backstory. The issue is what people do when presented with the truth, not why they do it. Hugo Mercier and Dan Sperber, 'Why do humans reason? Arguments for an argumentative theory,' *Behavioral and Brain Sciences*, 34, no. 2 (2011), 57–74.

21 Note, though, that Achen and Bartels make the distinct and more counterintuitive claim that people vote against their own *preferences*.

22 Lodge and Taber, 'Three steps toward a theory of motivated political reasoning,' 183–213. On different conceptions of bounded rationality, see: Gerd Gigerenzer, 'Striking a blow for sanity in theories of rationality' in Maxime Augier and James March, eds, *Models of a Man: Essays in Memory of Herbert A. Simon* (Cambridge, Mass: MIT Press, 2004), 389–409.

23 Christopher Achen and Larry Bartels, 'Democracy for realists: Holding up a mirror to the electorate,' *Juncture* 22, no. 4 (2016), 271.

24 The second half of their book sets out their 'group theory' of voting, but as it is developed there it does not offer detailed explanations for many of the negative findings about the folk theory which are set out in the first half of the book. Isabela Mares, 'A discussion of Christopher H. Achen and Larry M. Bartels' *Democracy for Realists*,' *Perspectives on Politics*, 159–60.

25 One useful heuristic is to read authors whom Chomsky cites. That would lead to the four mentioned in the text (among hundreds of others).

26 Edward S. Herman and Noam Chomsky, *Manufacturing Consent: The Political Economy of the Mass Media* (New York: Pantheon Books, 1988); Noam Chomsky, *Necessary Illusions: Thought Control in Democratic Societies* (London: Pluto, 1989); Edward S. Herman, 'The propaganda model: A retrospective,' *Against All Reason* (2003), 1, 1–14. For a brief introduction to Herman and Chomsky's propaganda model, see: Neil V. Smith and Nicholas Allott, *Chomsky: Ideas and Ideals*, 3rd ed. (Cambridge: Cambridge University Press, 2016), 314–9. There is a brief, sympathetic but critical discussion in Joshua Cohen and Joel Rogers, 'Knowledge, morality and hope: The social thought of Noam Chomsky,' *New Left Review* 187 (1991), 5–27.

27 Noam Chomsky, 'What makes mainstream media mainstream,' *Z Magazine* (October 1997).

28 Chomsky in Zane Wubbena, 'Breathing secondhand smoke: Gatekeeping for "good education", passive democracy, and the mass media. An interview with Noam Chomsky,' *Critical Education*, 6, no. 8 (2015). See also Noam Chomsky, *Letters From Lexington: Reflections on Propaganda*, 2nd ed. (London: Pluto Press, 2004), 4–7. Here Chomsky is paraphrasing and agreeing with Orwell's long-unpublished preface for *Animal Farm*. See https://www.bl.uk/collection-items/ orwells-proposed-introduction-to-animal-farm

29 Achen and Bartels, *Democracy for Realists*, 12.

30 Chomsky may agree with this. Certainly, he has often stressed that getting things done requires organised groups, e.g.: 'Being alone, you can't do anything – But if you join with other people you can make changes'. Noam Chomsky and David Barsamian, *Secrets, Lies, and Democracy* (Tucson, AZ: Odonian Press, 1994), 105–6.

31 Thomas Ferguson, *Golden Rule: The Investment Theory of Party Competition and the Logic of Money-Driven Political Systems* (Chicago: University of Chicago Press, 1995), 10.

32 Chomsky in Wubbena, 'Breathing secondhand smoke,' 3–4.

33 Other motivations/justifications for RoI would survive – see note 3 above.

34 Redlawsk, Civettini and Emmerson, 'The affective tipping point: Do motivated reasoners ever "get it"?' *Political Psychology*, 563–93. It is tempting to hope that as this essay is being written in late 2017 we are seeing that tipping point being reached vis-à-vis the Trump presidency by various prominent Republicans.

35 Redlawsk, Civettini and Emmerson, 'The affective tipping point: Do motivated reasoners ever "get it"?' *Political Psychology*, 563.

36 Alexis Grigorieff, Christopher Roth and Diego Ubfal, 'Does information change attitudes towards immigrants? Representative evidence from survey experiments,' *IZA Institute of Labor Economics Discussion Paper Series*, 10419 (2016), 1.

37 Giovanni Facchini, Yotam Margalit and Hiroyuki Nakata, 'Countering public opposition to immigration: The impact of information campaigns,' *IZA Institute of Labor Economics Discussion Paper Series*, 10420 (2016).

38 See Diana Mazzarella, Emmanuel Trouche, Hugo Mercier and Ira Noveck, 'Believing what you're told: Politeness and scalar inferences,' *Frontiers of Psychology* 9 (2018); and Diana Mazzarella, Robert Reinecke, Ira Noveck and Hugo Mercier, 'Saying, presupposing and implicating: How pragmatics modulates commitment,' *Journal of Pragmatics* 133 (2018).

39 See for example Brenda Major, Alison Blodorn and Gregory Major Blascovich, 'The threat of increasing diversity: Why many White Americans support Trump in the 2016 presidential election,' *Group Processes & Intergroup Relations* 21, no. 6 (2016). For overviews see Sheri Berman, 'Why identity politics benefits the right more than the left,' *The Guardian*, 14 July 2018; German Lopez, 'Research says there are ways to reduce racial bias. Calling people racist isn't one of them,' *Vox*, 14 August 2017.

40 Quoted in Lopez, 'Research says there are ways to reduce racial bias.'

4

The propaganda model and
the British nuclear weapons debate

Milan Rai

Intellectuals are in a position to expose the lies of governments, to analyze actions according to their causes and motives and often hidden intentions. In the western world, at least, they have the power that comes from political liberty, from access to information and freedom of expression. For a privileged minority, western democracy provides the leisure, the facilities, and the training to seek the truth lying hidden behind the veil of distortion and misrepresentation, ideology and class interest, through which the events of current history are presented to us. The responsibilities of intellectuals, then, are much deeper than what [Dwight] Macdonald calls the 'responsibility of people,' given the unique privileges that intellectuals enjoy.
– Noam Chomsky, 'The Responsibility of Intellectuals', 1967

This essay applies the Chomsky–Herman propaganda model of the mass media to the debate around nuclear weapons, especially in Britain. According to the propaganda model, the 'free press' serves the societal purpose of 'protecting privilege from the threat of public understanding and participation'.[1] Chomsky and Edward Herman describe the propaganda system as 'brainwashing under freedom':

A totalitarian state can be satisfied with lesser degrees of allegiance to required truths. It is sufficient that people obey; what they think is a secondary concern. But in a democratic political order, there is always the danger that independent thought might be translated into political action, so it is important to eliminate the threat at its root.[2]

Debate cannot be stilled, and indeed, in a properly functioning system of propaganda, it should not be, because it has a system-reinforcing character if constrained within proper bounds. What is essential is to set the bounds firmly. Controversy may rage as long as it adheres to the presuppositions that define the consensus of elites, and it should furthermore be encouraged within these bounds, thus helping to establish these doctrines as the very condition of thinkable thought while reinforcing the belief that freedom reigns.[3]

Since 1945, there have been several periods of intense public controversy over British nuclear weapons. This mainstream debate has had a 'system-reinforcing character' as it has kept to 'proper bounds'. As Chomsky observes, in any state religion, there are at least two basic principles. First, the Holy State is good. Officials and ministers make mistakes, sometimes through lack of knowledge, sometimes through lack of intelligence. Overall, though, the establishment is well-intentioned, despite the occasional bad apple. The second principle is that the Holy State is always acting defensively in nature.

How does this play out for the British nuclear weapons debate? According to these principles, Britain's nuclear weapons are there to defend Britain and other countries from attack. Chomsky suggests: 'A useful rule of thumb is this: If you want to learn something about the propaganda system, have a close look at the critics and their tacit assumptions. These typically constitute the doctrines of the state religion.'[4] If we look at the recent nuclear weapons debate in Britain, we find these kinds of remarks at the limits of 'responsible opinion'.

An editorial in the *Independent* back in 2005 said that the collapse of the Soviet Union 'has made the deterrence argument obsolete'. It went on: 'During the Cold War, nuclear weapons acted as a deterrent to aggression by other states.'[5] There was a similar critique from perhaps the most anti-militarist of the *Guardian*'s columnists. In 2013, Simon Jenkins said: 'It [the British nuclear deterrent] made no sense.' Keeping British nuclear weapons was 'irrational', 'mad', 'hare-brained', 'hypocritical', 'an irrelevance', 'absurd', and 'nonsense'. Jenkins wrote that Britain's nuclear weapons bore 'no reference to any plausible threat to Britain that could possibly merit their use'.[6]

What are some of the assumptions made by these establishment critics? First, British nuclear weapons are solely about defending the territory of Britain. Second, they're a defence against nuclear-armed enemies. Third, they are for retaliation after an attack on Britain (a threat which is supposed to make such an attack less likely). Fourth, Britain has not used its nuclear weapons.

These four assumptions are what the public thinks of as 'deterrence'. They have no basis in reality. In fact, Britain has used its nuclear weapons repeatedly.

Nuclear coercion

Daniel Ellsberg, the US military analyst who leaked the Pentagon's secret internal history of the Vietnam War, the Pentagon Papers, wrote in 1981:

> Again and again, generally in secret from the American public, US nuclear weapons have been used, for quite different purposes: in the precise way that a gun is used when you point it at someone's head in a direct confrontation, whether or not the trigger is pulled.[7]

Britain has used its nuclear weapons in the same way, repeatedly. Iraq has been threatened with British nuclear weapons on at least three occasions. In 1961, Britain created a phoney crisis in the Persian Gulf and mobilised its military forces to intimidate Iraq and the region. One element was the deployment of nuclear-capable Scimitar aircraft to the Gulf.[8] In Malta, British strategic nuclear bombers were placed on alert.[9] A right-wing British historian with intelligence connections, Anthony Verrier, later described the incident as an 'act of deterrence, in which the nuclear weapons system played a central, concealed role … directed against Nasser and, by extension, Russian ambitions in Arabia'.[10] Gamal Abdel Nasser was the nationalist president of Egypt. 'Russian ambitions in Arabia' is code for the forces of independent Arab nationalism generally, including in Iraq. Almost 30 years later, the US and British governments were determined to punish Iraq for invading Kuwait on 2 August 1990: eight days later, the British tabloid the *Daily Star* reported: 'Whitehall sources made it clear that the multinational forces would be ready to hit back with every means at their disposal … [including] using tactical nuclear weapons against [Iraqi] troops and tanks on the battlefield.'

On 30 September 1990, a senior British army officer with 7th Armoured Brigade warned on the front page of the *Observer* that if there were Iraqi chemical attacks, British forces would 'retaliate with battlefield nuclear forces'. On 26 October 1990, the *Daily Mail* reported: 'One senior minister said, "If we were prepared to use tactical nuclear weapons against the Russians, I can't see why we shouldn't be prepared to use them against Iraq".' On 13 November 1990, the senior *Guardian* journalist Hugo Young reported in the paper that he had heard a minister say that the war against Iraq might have to be ended with 'tactical nukes'. On 6 December 1990, the British Prime Minister, John Major, told television presenter David Frost that the use of nuclear weapons in the Gulf was 'not likely, remotely'. However, Major did not rule out the use of British nuclear weapons: it was a live policy option.

There were more nuclear threats in the run-up to the 2003 attack on Iraq. Then British Defence Secretary Geoff Hoon told the House of Commons Defence Select Committee on 20 March 2002 that states like Iraq 'can be absolutely confident that in the right conditions we would be willing to use our nuclear weapons'.[11] On 24 March 2002, Hoon told ITV's *Jonathan Dimbleby Show* that the government 'reserved the right' to use nuclear weapons if Britain or British troops were threatened by chemical or biological weapons. Hoon was asked about these nuclear threats in a House of Commons debate on 29 April 2002. The Defence Secretary said: 'ultimately, and in conditions of extreme self-defence, nuclear weapons would have to be used'. Hoon was pressed to explain but refused to clarify what this meant.

Other countries have also been subjected to British nuclear threats. In its early years, the British strategic nuclear force was airborne, carried by Valiant, Vulcan and Victor aircraft. These 'V-bombers' made hundreds of flights in the 1950s and 1960s across the British Empire. These global sorties were clearly not about 'defending' the homeland from being attacked by Russia.

In 1962, V-bombers attended independence ceremonies in Uganda and Jamaica.[12] When three Victors were sent back to Jamaica in 1966, they had 'more than decorative purposes' according to Andrew Brookes, historian of the V-bomber force and himself a former Vulcan pilot.[13] Brookes records that the Vulcans at RAF Waddington were committed in 1963 to 'dealing with conventional trouble in the Middle East', while their sister Victors in Cottesmore and Honington 'looked after the Far East'.[14] While these V-bombers might have been only carrying conventional weaponry in such conflicts, their deployment as strategic nuclear bombers outside Europe would have sent powerful and threatening nuclear signals to Britain's enemies.

Victors from Bomber Command were deployed to Singapore in December 1963, during Britain's 'confrontation' with Indonesia. According to Brookes, the nuclear bombers were kept in Singapore longer than usual, 'positioned to be seen as ready to eliminate Indonesia

Air Force capabilities if they launched air attacks.'[15] Brookes does not say what kind of bombs might have been used to carry out this 'elimination'.

Air Chief Marshal Sir David Lee wrote later of the nuclear-capable Victors: 'Their potential was well known to Indonesia and their presence did not go unnoticed.' He added: 'The knowledge of RAF strength and competence created a wholesome respect among Indonesia's leaders, and the deterrent effect of RAF air defence fighters, light bombers and V-bombers on detachment from Bomber Command was absolute'.[16] When the first Victors arrived at RAF Tengah in Singapore at the end of 1963, a storage unit had already been built at the base for 48 Red Beard nuclear bombs. The squadron then engaged in low-altitude nuclear bombing exercises.[17]

Here is the true meaning of deterrence. It is spelled out in the nuclear threats against Iraq, a non-nuclear weapon state in 1961, 1991 and 2003; in the V-bomber deployments throughout the British Empire in the 1950s and 1960s; in the commitment of Vulcans and Victors to 'deal with' the Middle East and the Far East (where there were no nuclear weapon states in 1963); and in the intimidation of Indonesia in the mid 1960s.

Respecting Britain's vital interests

Deterrence means cultivating a 'wholesome respect' for British violence in the lesser races who might interfere with British domination. Deterrence means preventing non-nuclear weapon states from using weapons or launching attacks that might defeat British expeditionary forces sent out into the global south. Deterrence means, if necessary, keeping the option open to use nuclear weapons to crush non-nuclear weapon states too tough to defeat by conventional means.

In other words:

- British nuclear weapons have not just been about 'defending Britain'; they have been 'used' right around the world.
- British nuclear weapons have been aimed at non-nuclear weapon states as well as nuclear-armed enemies.
- British nuclear weapons have been about nuclear intimidation and coercion as well as threatening nuclear retaliation.
- Britain *has* used its nuclear weapons – to threaten other countries during direct confrontations – and more widely.

This has been part of British nuclear policy since the beginning. The 1956 Defence White Paper, a public document, said: 'we have to be prepared for the outbreak of localised conflicts on a scale short of global war. In such limited wars the possible use of nuclear weapons cannot be excluded.' 'Localised conflicts' or 'limited wars' were wars in the global south, against opponents (either states or nationalist movements) who lacked nuclear weapons.

Nearly 40 years later, in November 1993, the then British Defence Secretary Malcolm Rifkind expressed the same view, with more cautious wording, again in a public speech:

> The ability to undertake a massive strike with strategic systems is not enough to ensure deterrence. An aggressor might, in certain circumstances, gamble on a lack of will ultimately to resort to such dire action. It is therefore important for the credibility of our deterrent that the United Kingdom also possesses the capability to undertake a more limited nuclear strike in order to induce a political decision to halt aggression by delivering an unmistakable message of our willingness to defend our vital interests to the utmost.[18]

The 2010–15 Coalition government said: 'The purpose of our nuclear weapons is to deter an attack on the UK, our vital interests or our allies'[19] – three distinct entities or concepts. Looking through the documentary record, it is clear that 'vital interests' relate to British financial and economic interests, critical raw materials and trade routes – outside Europe.[20] All of this is a matter of public record, and yet these important facts did not enter the fierce debates about British nuclear weapons possession in the 1980s, or more recently about the replacement of the Trident nuclear weapons system.

Propaganda and deterrence

Earlier, in relation to the 1991 nuclear threats against Iraq, I referred to a lot of material that appeared in British newspapers. How can the mainstream media really be a kind of propaganda system if such disturbing facts were reported, sometimes prominently, in mainstream newspapers? Herman and Chomsky comment:

> That the media provide some information about an issue ... proves absolutely nothing about the adequacy or accuracy of media

coverage. The media do in fact suppress a great deal of information, but even more important is the way they present a particular fact – its placement, tone, and frequency of repetition – and the framework of analysis in which it is placed.[21]

Chomsky explains that:

> The enormous amount of material that is produced in the media and books makes it possible for a really assiduous and committed researcher to gain a fair picture of the real world by cutting through the mass of misrepresentation and fraud to the nuggets hidden within.[22]

> That a careful reader, looking for a fact can sometimes find it, with diligence and a sceptical eye, tells us nothing about whether that fact received the attention and context it deserved, whether it was intelligible to most readers, or whether it was effectively distorted or suppressed.[23]

The debate over the morality of nuclear retaliation, a debate which raged fiercely during the upsurge of the 1980s, has been a damaging distraction from the real issues and the inconvenient truths of British nuclear history and policy. Much of the challenge from the peace movement has reinforced state propaganda by focusing on hypothetical retaliation in the future rather than actual nuclear intimidation and coercion in the past and the present. The heart of the matter is that British national security policy has not been driven by a concern for national security, but by a commitment to dominate, to control 'vital interests'. In parallel, the engagement of the mainstream media with these issues has been driven not by a concern for truth but by a commitment to serve power and privilege.

Notes

1   Noam Chomsky, *Necessary Illusions* (Pluto Press, 1989), 14.
2   Noam Chomsky, *The Washington Connection and Third World Fascism* (Montréal: Black Rose Books, 1979), 66–83.
3   Chomsky, *Necessary Illusions* (Pluto Press, 1989), 48.
4   Noam Chomsky, *The Chomsky Reader* (Serpent's Tail, 1988), 126.
5   'Hypocrisy and the nuclear deterrent,' *The Independent*, 2 May 2005.
6   Simon Jenkins, 'This £100bn. armageddon weapon won't make us one jot safer,' *The Guardian*, 25 September 2013.
7   Daniel Ellsberg, 'Call to mutiny,' in *Protest and Survive*, eds Edward Thompson and Dan Smith (Monthly Review, 1981).

8   Adel Darwish and Gregory Alexander, *Unholy Babylon: The Secret History of Saddam's War* (London: Gollancz, 1991), 33.
9   Andrew Brookes, *Force V: The History of Britain's Airborne Deterrent* (London: Jane's, 1982), 141.
10 Anthony Verrier, *Through the Looking Glass: British Foreign Policy in an Age of Illusions* (London: Jonathan Cape, 1983), 171.
11 Kim Sengupta, 'Hoon warns rogue states to expect nuclear retaliation,' *The Independent*, 21 March 2002.
12 Ministry of Defence, *Statement on Defence 1963* (HMSO, 1963), para. 59.
13 Brookes, *Force V* (1982), 140.
14 Brookes, *Force V* (1982), 140.
15 Brookes, *Force V* (1982), 138.
16 David Lee, *Eastward: A History of the RAF in the Far East, 1945–72* (London: HMSO, 1984), 213.
17 Tom Rhodes, 'Britain kept secret nuclear weapons in Singapore and Cyprus,' *Sunday Times*, 31 December 2000.
18 Malcolm Rifkind, 'UK Defence Strategy: A continuing role for nuclear weapons?' in *Brassey's Defence Yearbook 1994* (London: Brassey's, 1994).
19 Ministry of Defence, '2010 to 2015 government policy: UK nuclear deterrent' (London: HMSO, updated 8 May 2015).
20 See: Ministry of Defence, *Statement on the Defence Estimates 1995: Stable Forces in a Strong Britain* (London: HMSO, 1995), 9.
21 Edward Herman and Noam Chomsky, 'Propaganda mill: The media churn out the "official line",' *The Progressive*, June 1988, 15.
22 Noam Chomsky, *Towards a New Cold War: Essays on the Current Crisis and How We Got There* (Great Britain: Sinclair Browne, 1982), 14.
23 Herman and Chomsky, 'Propaganda mill,' 15.

5

Speaking truth to power – from within the heart of the empire

Chris Knight

For over 50 years, Noam Chomsky has been speaking truth to power not from a safe distance – anyone can do that – but from right up close and personal within his own workplace, the Massachusetts Institute of Technology (MIT). One of the intellectuals singled out by Chomsky in 'The Responsibility of Intellectuals' was a professor from MIT, Walt Rostow. By the time Chomsky published his classic essay, Rostow had become national security adviser to President Lyndon Johnson. In the essay, Chomsky explicitly condemned his former MIT colleague as a principal architect of the ongoing 'butchery in Vietnam'.[1]

Chomsky was certainly aware that MIT employed a range of other academics and intellectuals who were similarly implicated in the crimes of the US military. Although Chomsky tends to play down the internal conflicts and challenges at his university, the truth is that denouncing his fellow academics cannot have been straightforward or easy. In this contribution I will focus, in particular, on three especially powerful figures at MIT: Jerome Wiesner, John Deutch and James McCormack.

Jerome Wiesner and the Pentagon

To allow a full appreciation of Chomsky's institutional position, let me take you back to his first job interview in 1955. It was for a post in a military lab at a time when the Cold War was at its height. The successful applicant would join a team at MIT's Research Laboratory of Electronics (RLE) working on machine translation, a project heavily funded by the Pentagon with military applications in mind. The interviewer that day was Jerome Wiesner, then the director of the RLE and one of the most influential military scientists in the country. Explaining his interest in the young linguist, Wiesner recalls: 'Professor Bill Locke suggested we use computers to do automatic translation, so we hired Noam Chomsky and Yehoshua Bar-Hillel to work on it.'[2] Illustrating his dry sense of humour, Chomsky recalls what he said to Wiesner in that interview:

> I told him, I don't think the project makes any sense. The only way to solve this problem is brute force. What's going to be understood about language is not really going to help and I'm just not interested, so I'm not going to do it. He thought that was a pretty good answer. So he hired me on the machine translation project. But mainly to do what I felt like.[3]

We may regret that Chomsky never got to write a beginner's manual for handling job interviews. 'Always turn the tables' might well have been his advice!

To savour the ironies of Chomsky's employment at the Research Laboratory of Electronics, it helps to know more about Jerome Wiesner. In terms of US military policy, Chomsky remembers the RLE director as a dove: 'He was on the extreme dovish side of the … Kennedy administration. But he never really accepted the fact that the students and the activists considered him a kind of a collaborator.'[4] This double-edged evaluation suggests to me that Chomsky knew from the outset about Wiesner's collaboration with the Pentagon, but out of respect for his senior colleague left it to others to condemn him on those grounds.

A specialist in communications engineering, from 1952 to 1980 Wiesner rose from director of the RLE to provost and then president of MIT, in effect making him Chomsky's boss for over 20 years.[5] Wiesner also played a leading role in setting up MIT's linguistics programme. As Chomsky says: 'Modern linguistics developed as part of what's sometimes called the "cognitive revolution" of the 1950s, actually to a large extent here [in the RLE], thanks initially to Jerry Wiesner's initiatives.'[6]

It is easy to see why MIT's students considered Wiesner 'a kind of collaborator'. After all, it was Wiesner who, in the 1950s, had brought nuclear missile research to MIT.[7] Wiesner, moreover, was openly proud of the fact that the RLE – centrally situated on MIT's campus – had made 'major scientific and technical contributions to the continuing and growing military technology of the United States.'[8]

In 1971, the US Army's Office of the Chief of Research and Development published a list of what it called 'just a few examples' of the 'many RLE research contributions that have had military applications'.

The list included 'beam-shaping antennas', 'helical antennas', 'microwave filters', 'ionospheric communication', 'missile guidance', 'atomic clocks', 'signal detection', 'communication theory', 'information and coding theory', 'human sensor augmentation' and 'neuroelectric signals'.[9] Given the military significance of all such projects, Chomsky would have had his work cut out disentangling his own theories about language from any possible military use.

Wiesner's contribution to the US military, however, was far greater than his involvement with the RLE. One major achievement, he reminds us, was that he 'helped get the United States ballistic missile program established in the face of strong opposition from the civilian and military leaders of the Air Force and Department of Defense'. He adds that he was also 'a proponent of the Polaris missile system, the ballistic missile early warning system, and the satellite reconnaissance systems'.[10] By 1961, Wiesner had become President Kennedy's chief science adviser and it was from this influential position that he was able to insist that nuclear missile development and procurement 'must all be accelerated'.[11] To justify this military build-up, Kennedy invoked the myth of America's military weakness compared with the Soviet Union – the total fiction of a 'missile gap' that, according to Wiesner's own account, 'I helped invent'.[12]

After Kennedy's assassination, Wiesner's power declined. However, he was still able to contribute to the US war machine by bringing together a team of leading scientists – including 11 from MIT – in a project to design and deploy a vast barrier of sensors, mines and cluster bombs along the border between North and South Vietnam, the so-called McNamara Line.[13] Wiesner's longstanding involvement with nuclear decision-making, and his consequent awareness of just how flawed and dishonest the whole process was, did lead him to criticise the unrestrained stockpiling of nuclear missiles, particularly those equipped with multiple warheads. But this change of heart did not stop him from continuing to run laboratories at MIT dedicated to research on just such developments.[14]

Wiesner stepped down as MIT's president in 1980, but what the university's representatives call its 'deep relationship' with the Pentagon continues to this day.[15] Since 1980, MIT's on-campus research has included work on missiles, space defence, warships, nuclear submarines, IEDs, robots, drones and 'battle suits'.[16]

So, the individual who gave Chomsky his first academic post, and who was his boss for over 20 years, was one of the chief designers of the military machine whose crimes Chomsky so eloquently condemned in 'The Responsibility of Intellectuals'. The moment he accepted his position at MIT, therefore, Chomsky became immersed in a world whose primary technological mission he detested. And, as more and more students became politically radicalised during the 1960s, he would certainly have known about their attitude to MIT, which was succinctly expressed in this 1969 passage from the radical newspaper *The Old Mole*:

> MIT isn't a center for scientific and social research to serve humanity. It's a part of the US war machine. Into MIT flow over $100 million a year in Pentagon research and development funds, making it the tenth largest Defense Department R&D contractor in the country. MIT's purpose is to provide research, consulting services and trained personnel for the US government and the major corporations – research, services, and personnel which enable them to maintain their control over the people of the world.[17]

John Deutch and the CIA

The second figure in my narrative is John Deutch who, as MIT's provost, brought biological warfare research to the university in the 1980s.[18] Like Wiesner, Deutch's influence ranged well beyond MIT. For example, he played a key role in the Pentagon's chemical weapons strategy, in its deployment of MX missiles and in its 1994 Nuclear Posture Review.[19] Deutch's passion for nuclear weaponry was neatly summed up by his wife, Patricia, when she explained: 'John loves nukes'.[20]

By 1994, Deutch had failed in one of his ambitions – to become MIT president – but he had succeeded in becoming Deputy Defense Secretary. Then, in 1995, Bill Clinton made him Director of the Central Intelligence Agency. Shortly afterwards, Chomsky was asked about his relationship with Deutch:

> We were actually friends and got along fine, although we disagreed on about as many things as two human beings can disagree about. I liked him. We got along very well together. He's very honest, very direct. You know where you stand with him. We talked to each other. When we had disagreements, they were open, sharp, clear, honestly dealt with. I found it fine. I had no problem with him. I was one of the very few people on the faculty, I'm told, who was supporting his candidacy for the President of MIT.[21]

Before the 1990s, during the Cold War, the CIA had focused as much on political as on military intelligence gathering. This was because using political intelligence to avoid nuclear war with the Soviet Union was far preferable to fighting such a war – a war that could only lead to disaster for everyone. But US victory in the 1991 Gulf War showed that, with the end of the Cold War, conventional wars were once again winnable. The CIA now began working more closely with the Pentagon in order to help them fight wars in the Middle East and elsewhere. And, from 1995, Deutch's new team at the agency emphasised what they called 'Support for Military Operations' and 'Tactical Intelligence for the Warfighter'.[22]

Had Chomsky been able to converse with Deutch about this, there would undoubtedly have been still more 'open, sharp, clear' disagreements between the two friends. But, as far as the readers of the *New York Times* were concerned, all they knew was what Chomsky said publicly – which was that Deutch 'has more honesty and integrity than anyone I've ever met in academic life, or any other life. If somebody's got to be running the CIA, I'm glad it's him.'[23]

Despite these comments, I doubt that Chomsky was ever truly comfortable rubbing shoulders with Deutch, any more than with the numerous other war scientists conducting research at MIT. When anti-war student protests swept MIT in 1969, Chomsky took the opportunity to say what he really thought about some of his professional colleagues:

> I think that MIT is going to have to take seriously something that it never has in the past, namely, the social, political, and historical context in which scientific and technical development takes place. It is appalling that a person can come through an MIT education and say the kinds of things that were quoted in the *New York Times*. ... One student said, right along straight Nazi scientist lines: 'What I'm designing may one day be used to kill millions of people. I don't care. That's not my responsibility. I'm given an interesting technological problem and I get enjoyment out of solving it.' You know perfectly well that we can name twenty faculty members who've said the same thing.[24]

In these words – at this time – Chomsky made abundantly clear what he thought: some of his colleagues, faculty members at MIT, were acting 'right along straight Nazi scientist lines'. The point was reinforced by Chomsky's friend and political ally, the student leader Michael Albert, when he described the MIT campus on Boston's Charles River as 'Dachau on the Charles', adding that 'MIT's victims burned in the fields of Vietnam.'[25]

Such comments may seem extreme. But they are surely appropriate when we consider that during this period, MIT's laboratories were researching helicopter design, radar, smart bombs and counter-insurgency techniques all intended to be used in a horrific war in Vietnam, Laos and Cambodia in which at least two million people died.[26]

James McCormack and the MITRE Corporation

Another important administrator at MIT was Air Force General James McCormack. Before coming to the university, McCormack had played a leading role in the creation of the US' entire post-war nuclear arsenal, including the development of the hydrogen bomb. In 1949, McCormack saw almost no limit to this new weapon's monstrous potential, telling his political masters in Washington that 'if all of the theory turned out, you can have it any size up to the sun'.[27]

In 1958 McCormack became a vice-president at MIT, where he supervised various research projects, including the Center for Communication Studies, with which both Wiesner and Chomsky were involved.[28] McCormack also played a key role in setting up an important offshoot of MIT called the MITRE Corporation.

It was this MITRE Corporation that went on to develop various lethal hi-tech devices for the McNamara Line in Vietnam and whose scientists (including a number of Chomsky's students) tried hard to use Chomsky's linguistics in their war-related research.[29] One can only imagine how conflicted Chomsky must have felt when, from 1963 to 1965, he found himself employed as a consultant to MITRE. Apparently, Chomsky's role was to advise the corporation's linguists on how to use his theories for a computer-based program 'to establish natural language as an operational language for command and control'.[30]

One of Chomsky's students at MITRE, Barbara Partee, has told me that this employment of linguists was justified to the Air Force on the grounds that 'in the event of a nuclear war, the generals would be underground with some computers trying to manage things, and that it would probably be easier to teach computers to understand English than to teach the generals to program'.[31] Partee says she is unsure whether anyone really believed this justification at the time yet recalls that the Air Force did need to be offered some plausible reason why they were spending so much money on Chomsky's linguistics.

In the end, the MITRE Corporation never did manage to make Chomsky's theories work, as was admitted by former Air Force Colonel Anthony Debons in 1971:

> Language is a direct concern to military command and control for several reasons. Understanding the structure of a language provides the means for developing a machine language which facilitates the man–machine interaction required in such systems. Much of the research conducted at MIT by Chomsky and his colleagues [has] direct application to the efforts undertaken by military scientists to develop such languages for computer operations in military command and control systems. By and large, the theoretical studies made in this area, however, have not as yet led to any appreciable success in the development of a natural language for computer applications.[32]

Clearly, Chomsky's involvement with MITRE was bringing him dangerously close to direct collusion with the US military. While others may have experienced few moral qualms, Chomsky was different.

To appreciate his sensitivities, we need only recall his deep concern in 1959, when his wife, the linguist Carol Chomsky, began working on an air defense project at MIT's Lincoln Laboratory. The project was intended to enable 'the business executive, the military commander and the scientist' to communicate with computers in 'natural language'.[33] According to the project's administrative head, Bert Green, 'Noam was very nervous about our work, and met with me to voice his concerns. Since the work was being done at an Air Force lab, he believed that ... we were really working on voice activated command and control systems.'[34]

In this particular case – at least for a while – Chomsky seems to have put any worries to one side and, when he first began working at MITRE, he doesn't appear to have flagged up his political dissidence.[35] He must have continued to feel uneasy about the military, especially its role in Vietnam, but as he said to a TV interviewer in 1974: 'I didn't become really actively engaged in opposing the war until about 1964, 1965.'[36] In another interview, he said that by 1964 he had reached a point when:

> I couldn't keep quiet any longer, and I started to give talks [about Vietnam]. ... It got so horrible over there that I couldn't look at myself in the mirror anymore.[37]

As he recalled, in yet another account of this period: 'I was deeply immersed in the work I was doing. It was intellectually exciting, and all sorts of fascinating avenues of research were opening up.' But, with what he called 'considerable reluctance', he now resolved to divert his energies into anti-war activism.[38]

By the autumn of 1965, Chomsky's consultancy work for MITRE seems to have come to an end. Having already spoken at unofficial teach-ins during the summer, in a striking shift in his academic priorities, Chomsky now began running an official course at MIT called 'Intellectuals and Social Change'. He also became an adviser to MIT's anti-Vietnam War committee, although such activism only ever involved what he calls 'a very small group of faculty'.[39] This turn to activism meant that Chomsky began writing about topics which, previously, he says, 'I never would have thought of writing about.'[40] And in the spring of 1966, aged 37, he published what appears to have been his first political article since childhood, an early version of 'The Responsibility of Intellectuals'.[41]

In this and subsequent writings, Chomsky has never, to my knowledge, made any reference to his involvement with the MITRE Corporation. But, when referring to the military work of fellow professors at MIT, he has expressed concern that student protests against such work may be misdirected:

> I think that a good deal of the energy of the student movement is flowing into irrelevant directions. There are tasks to which student agitation might be directed, such as formally severing relations with the IDA (Institute for Defense Analyses), or restructuring the universities, or putting people on committees, and even ending defense work. Many of these things could be undertaken without leading to any objective change in the character of the society and what it does. That worries me very much. You see, at a place like MIT people like the chairman of the political science department learned long ago that you don't do your really unspeakable work in your capacity as a college professor. You do that work in your capacity as a member of a corporation which has been set up for that purpose.[42]

MITRE was, of course, a classic example of such a corporation.

Chomsky has been very candid about his personal failure to act earlier to oppose the onslaught against Vietnam, openly referring to 'those of us who stood by in silence and apathy as this catastrophe slowly took shape.'[43] In the 1969 introduction to his first political book, *American Power and the New Mandarins*, he wrote:

No one who involved himself in anti-war activities as late as 1965, as I did, has any reason for pride or satisfaction. This opposition was ten or fifteen years too late.[44]

Despite these heartfelt regrets, Chomsky was determined to continue his linguistics research at MIT. But from this point on, he felt morally impelled to clarify that his work was restricted to pure science. His linguistic theories had always been highly abstract but he now needed to stress that if his military sponsors found his models to be unworkable, that did not bother him at all. He would press on with models of language so utterly abstract and ideal – so completely removed from social usage, communication or any kind of technological application – that they were never likely to work for weapons 'command and control' or indeed for any other military purpose.[45]

Noam Chomsky and responsibility

Chomsky was always a committed anti-militarist and, equally, a libertarian, which for him meant giving free rein to the conscience of each individual scientist to pursue their chosen path. Here, he adopted what he himself termed 'a pretty extreme position' – 'one that might be hard to defend had anyone ever criticized it'.[46] Chomsky even went so far as to say that he 'supported the rights of American war criminals not only to speak and teach but also to conduct their research, on grounds of academic freedom, at a time when their work was being used to murder and destroy'.[47]

But wasn't this position dangerously close to what Chomsky himself condemned as thinking 'along straight Nazi scientist lines'? As if aware of the dilemma, he explained in 1983: 'I would stop doing what I was doing if I discovered that I was engaged in an area of scientific research that I thought, under existing social conditions, would lead to, say, oppression, destruction, and pain.'[48] Yet even on this point, he seemed unsure. Asked point-blank whether he might have conducted research in nuclear physics back in 1929 – when it was already clear that it might lead to an atomic bomb – Chomsky replied:

I don't think a glib answer is possible. Still, if you ask me specifically, I'm sure that my answer would have been yes. I would have done the work just out of interest and curiosity and with the hope that things would somehow work out.[49]

So, even where certain scientists are clearly criminals, explained Chomsky, this does not necessarily mean that they should be prevented from continuing their work. Rather than relying on the restrictions imposed by wider society, all of us should accept that 'people have a responsibility for the foreseeable consequences of their actions, and therefore have the responsibility of thinking about the research they undertake and what it might lead to under existing conditions'.[50]

Some critics of the Vietnam War did view Chomsky's employment at MIT as weakening his moral standing. Having just read 'The Responsibility of Intellectuals', the philosopher and literary critic George Steiner wrote privately to its author with some difficult questions:

> STEINER: Will Noam Chomsky announce that he will stop teaching at MIT or anywhere in this country so long as torture and napalm go on? ... Will he even resign from a university very largely implicated in the kind of 'strategic studies' he so rightly scorns? The intellectual is responsible. What then shall he do?

> CHOMSKY: I have given a good bit of thought to the specific suggestions that you put forth ... leaving the country or resigning from MIT, which is, more than any other university, associated with activities of the department of 'defense.' ... Perhaps this is a rationalization, but my own conclusion is that it is, for the present, not improper for an anti-war American intellectual to stay here and oppose the government, in as outspoken a way as he can, inside the country, and within the universities that have accepted a large measure of complicity in war and repression. ... As to MIT, I think that its involvement in the war effort is tragic and indefensible. One should, I feel, resist this subversion of the university in every possible way.[51]

However, when Steiner had this correspondence published in the *New York Review of Books*, Chomsky backed away from such outright public criticism of MIT. In a subsequent letter to the *Review*, published in April 1967, Chomsky decided to 'reformulate' his earlier criticism: 'This statement is unfair, and needs clarification. As far as I know, MIT as an institution has no involvement in the war effort. Individuals at MIT, as elsewhere, have a direct involvement, and that is what I had in mind.'[52] It is relevant to note here that by this point, MIT's managers had given Chomsky a named professorship which, as he recalls, 'isolated me from the alumni and government pressures.' But, despite this, his retraction suggests that he was still facing pressure from somewhere, presumably from his own colleagues at MIT.[53]

When, in 1970, in the aftermath of student unrest, MIT held a major art symposium, one anti-war commentator dismissed the event as little more than 'camouflage for the "military-industrial complex"'.[54] MIT's remarkable tolerance for Chomsky's activism was, doubtless, yet another way for the Pentagon-sponsored university to 'camouflage' its real role in this complex. But that hardly means we should therefore dismiss Chomsky's decades of tireless anti-militarist activism.

Having said that, Chomsky himself is modest about this political work. Whereas his linguistic research could only have been pursued by a scientist with his specific capacities, he claims that his activist contributions are just common sense and could have been produced by almost anyone. He feels there is nothing *intellectually* exciting about, say, explaining the rise of Richard Nixon or Donald Trump. The reasons for such political developments are clear enough. Equally, it needs no great *theoretical* insight to conclude that killing civilians during wartime is morally wrong, or that prohibiting other countries from stockpiling nuclear weapons is richly ironic if you are doing precisely that yourself. Chomsky feels that such things should be obvious to anyone who is ready to think a little.

But if we accept this argument, it raises the question why so many people – including myself – find his political contributions so inspiring. My preferred explanation differs from Chomsky's own.

Noam is by no means just another US citizen. The US military and foreign policy establishment is not known for its sensitive moral conscience. But insofar as that conscience has existed for the past half century, Noam Chomsky has been it. This is surely why he enjoys such immense moral standing.

Many of us try to speak the truth, but few of us can count among our friends or colleagues advisers to US presidents or a director of the CIA. Coming from within the belly of the beast, Chomsky's words have special resonance. As both an insider and an outsider of the US military-industrial complex, he knows what he is talking about. What he says may sometimes appear obvious – especially to those of us living outside the US – but the problem is that such things are rarely said by figures with such inside knowledge and corresponding authority. Chomsky breaks the mould by speaking truth to power even when denouncing the activities of his own colleagues and friends.

5.1 Jerome Wiesner (far left), the scientist who recruited Chomsky to MIT, with Defense Secretary Robert McNamara and Vice-President Lyndon Johnson in the White House, 1961. (Courtesy of White House Photographs. John F. Kennedy Presidential Library and Museum, Boston. Photo: Abbie Rowe)

5.2 Preparation for nuclear war: the SAGE (Semi-Automatic Ground Environment) air defense system. In the 1960s, the Pentagon sponsored linguists in the hope of making such computer systems easier to use. (Photo: Andreas Feininger/The LIFE Picture Collection/Getty Images)

5.3 Protesters demonstrate outside one of MIT's nuclear missile laboratories, November 1969. (Courtesy of MIT Museum, Cambridge, MA)

5.4 Police disperse protesters, November 1969. (Courtesy of MIT Museum, Cambridge, MA)

5.5 Building the US nuclear stockpile: General James McCormack (in uniform), a future vice-president at MIT, next to Robert Oppenheimer (second on the left), on the way to Los Alamos, 1947. (Photo: US Dept of Energy, Washington, DC)

5.6 Former MIT Provost, and future Director of the CIA, John Deutch at the Pentagon. (Photo: James E. Jackson, 12 April 1993. US Department of Defense, Washington, DC. The appearance of US Department of Defense (DoD) visual information does not imply or constitute DoD endorsement)

Notes

1   Noam Chomsky, *American Power and the New Mandarins* (New York: Vintage Books, 1969), 357.
2   Simson Garfinkel, 'Building 20, a survey' (No date), http://ic.media.mit.edu/projects/JBW/ARTICLES/SIMSONG.HTM (accessed January 2017).
3   Noam Chomsky, 'Infinite history project,' interview by Karen Arenson, 29 May 2009. https://archive.org/details/NoamChomsky-InfiniteHistoryProject-2009/
4   Noam Chomsky, 'Language: The cognitive revolutions' (20th Killian Award Lecture), filmed 8 April 1992 at MIT, Cambridge, MA. https://infinitehistory.mit.edu/video/20th-killian-award-lecture%E2%80%94noam-chomsky (accessed January 2018).
5   Walter Rosenblith (ed.), *Jerry Wiesner: Scientist, Statesman, Humanist: Memories and Memoirs* (Cambridge, MA: MIT Press, 2003), 524–34.
6   Kathryn O'Neill, 'Scientific reunion commemorates 50 years of linguistics at MIT,' MIT Linguistics website, https://shass.mit.edu/news/news-2011-scientific-reunion-commemorates-50-years-linguistics-mit (accessed November 2018); Chomsky, 'Language: The cognitive revolutions' (1992).
7   Jerome Wiesner, 'War and peace in the nuclear age; bigger bang for the buck, a; interview with Jerome Wiesner, [1],' WGBH Media Library and Archives (1986), http://openvault.wgbh.org/catalog/V_DD3A084107E94632B6AD7D428A966304 (accessed March 2017), 2 mins.
     Chomsky was well aware of what was going on at his university. As he said, 'I'm at MIT, so I'm always talking to the scientists who work on missiles for the Pentagon.' Or again: 'There was extensive weapons research on the MIT campus … In fact, a good deal of the [nuclear] missile guidance technology was developed right on the MIT campus and in laboratories run by the university.' Noam Chomsky, *Understanding Power* (New York: The New Press, 2002), 10; Noam Chomsky in *Language and Politics*, ed. Carlos Otero (Montréal: Black Rose Books, 1988), 233–50.
8   Jerome Wiesner, 'A successful experiment,' *Naval Research Reviews* 21, no. 7 (July 1966), 4.
9   'Tri-Services honor MIT achievements in military electronics research and development,' *Army Research and Development News Magazine* 12, no. 4 (Washington: HQ Department of the Army, July–August 1971), 68.
10 Jerome Wiesner, 'Prof. Wiesner explains,' *Chicago Tribune*, 29 June 1969, 24, http://scienceandrevolution.org/blog/2018/1/14/chomskys-supervisors-at-mit-wiesner-and-mccormack (accessed November 2018). Wiesner also had an enduring influence on British nuclear policy when he advised President Kennedy 'to sell Polaris missiles, excluding warheads, at a cost of about $1 million each to the UK'. Andrew Priest, *Kennedy, Johnson and NATO: Britain, America and the Dynamics of Alliance, 1962–68* (London and New York: Routledge, 2006), 42–4.
11 Jerome Wiesner, *Report to the President-Elect of the Ad Hoc Committee on Space* (1961), http://www.hq.nasa.gov/office/pao/History/report61.html (accessed September 2016).
12 Donald Brennan, *ABM, Yes or No? Center Occasional Papers* 2, no. 2 (Santa Barbara, CA: Center for the Study of Democratic Institutions, 1969), 33; David Snead, *The Gaither Committee, Eisenhower, and the Cold War* (Columbus, OH: Ohio State University Press, 1999), 118.
13 Walter Rosenblith (ed.), *Jerry Wiesner* (2003), 103; *New York Times*, 'A secret seminar,' 2 July 1971, 12, https://www.nytimes.com/1971/07/02/archives/a-secret-seminar.html; Anne Finkbeiner, *The Jasons: The Secret History of Science's Post-War Elite* (New York: Penguin, 2007), 65–6, 75–6; Bob Feldman, 'Columbia University's IDA Jason Project 1960s work – Part 9' (2008), http://bfeldman68.blogspot.co.uk/2008/04/columbia-universitys-ida-jason-project.html (accessed December 2016); Sarah Bridger, *Scientists at War: the Ethics of Cold War Weapons Research* (Cambridge, MA: Harvard University Press, 2015), ch. 5.
14 Andrew Hamilton, 'M.I.T.: March 4 revisited amid political turmoil,' *Science* 3924, 13 March 1970, 1475; 'MIT and social responsibility,' *Technology Review*, June 1970, 82.
15 United Press International, 'MIT students allege defense conflict' (1989), http://www.upi.com/Archives/1989/06/02/MIT-students-allege-defense-conflict/2508612763200/ (accessed February 2017).
16 Daniel J. Glenn, 'A crack in the dome – Twenty years later, MIT still doing military research projects,' *The Tech* 109, no. 6, 24 February 1989, 5; Bryan Bender, 'MIT team helps disarm bombs,' *The Tech*, 126, no. 7, 28 February 2006, 13; Jennifer Chu, 'MIT cheetah robot lands

the running jump,' *MIT News*, 29 May 2015, http://news.mit.edu/2015/cheetah-robot-lands-running-jump-0529 (accessed February 2017); Jennifer Chu, 'Driving drones can be a drag,' *MIT News*, 14 November 2012, http://news.mit.edu/2012/boredom-and-unmanned-aerial-vehicles-1114 (accessed February 2017); *MIT News*, 'Ocean engineering students set stage for a smarter fleet,' *MIT News*, 14 August 2013, http://news.mit.edu/2013/ocean-engineering-students-set-stage-for-a-smarter-fleet (accessed February 2017); US Department of Defense, 'Department of Defense announces successful micro-drone demonstration,' Press release, 9 January 2017, https://dod.defense.gov/News/News-Releases/News-Release-View/Article/1044811/department-of-defense-announces-successful-micro-drone-demonstration/; Alan Leo, 'The soldier of tomorrow,' *MIT Technology Review*, 20 March 2002; Thomas Ippolito, 'Effects of variation of uranium enrichment on nuclear submarine reactor design,' MSc thesis, MIT, 1990.

17 Immanuel Wallerstein and Paul Starr, eds, *The University Crisis Reader* (New York: Random House, 1972), 240–1.

18 This claim comes from the student newspaper, *The Thistle*. 'An open letter to President Vest,' and 'Who is John Deutch?' *The Thistle* 9, no. 7, http://web.mit.edu/activities/thistle/v9/9.07/tv9.07.html (accessed 2 April 2017); Anu Vedantham, 'Teach-in focuses on research and activism,' *The Tech* 109, no. 9, 7 March 1989, 2, http://tech.mit.edu/V109/PDF/V109-N9.pdf (accessed November 2018); Thomas T. Huang, 'Examining John Deutch's Pentagon connections,' *The Tech* 108, no. 26, 27 May 1988, 2, 11, http://tech.mit.edu/V108/PDF/V108-N26.pdf (accessed November 2018); Rich Cowan, 'Military provost,' *Science for the People*, March–April 1988, 6, http://science-for-the-people.org/wp-content/uploads/2015/07/SftPv20n2s.pdf (accessed November 2018).

19 John Deutch, 'Myth and reality in chemical warfare,' *Chemical and Engineering News* 60, no. 1 (February 1982), 24–5; Brent Scowcroft, *Report of the President's Commission on Strategic Forces* (Washington, DC: The White House, 1983), frontispiece, 20–21; Brent Scowcroft, John Deutch and James Woolsey, 'A small, survivable, mobile ICBM,' *Washington Post*, 26 December 1986, 23; John Deutch, 'The decision to modernize US intercontinental ballistic missiles,' *Science* 244, no. 4911 (1989), 1445–50; UPI, 'MIT students allege defense conflict' (1989); Bill Keller, 'Pentagon panel said to support building of small mobile missile,' *New York Times*, 2 February 1986, 1; Kathleen Bailey, 'Why we have to keep the bomb,' *Bulletin of the Atomic Scientists* (January 1995), 31.

20 Thomas Powers, 'Computer security; The whiz kids versus the old boys,' *New York Times Magazine*, 3 December 2000.

21 Noam Chomsky, *Class Warfare: Interviews with David Barsamian* (London: Pluto Press, 1996), 101.

22 Loch Johnson, *Secret Agencies: U.S. Intelligence in a Hostile World* (New Haven and London: Yale University Press, 1998), 50–1.

23 Tim Weiner, 'The C.I.A.'s most important mission: itself,' *New York Times*, 10 December 1995.

24 Noam Chomsky, *Chomsky on Democracy and Education*, ed. Carlos P. Otero (New York: RoutledgeFalmer, 2003), 290. For more on MIT's anti-war movement and the university's attempts to contain this movement using the Pounds Commission report and other administrative changes, see Chris Knight, *Decoding Chomsky: Science and Revolutionary Politics* (London and New Haven: Yale University Press, 2018), ch.4.

25 Michael Albert, *Remembering Tomorrow: From the Politics of Opposition to What We Are For* (New York: Seven Stories Press, 2006), 9.

26 Albert, *Remembering Tomorrow* (2006), 97–9; Nick Turse, *Kill Anything that Moves: The Real American War in Vietnam* (New York: Picador, 2013), 12–13.

27 Richard Hewlett and Francis Duncan, *Atomic Shield: A History of the United States Atomic Energy Commission, Vol. 2, 1947/1952* (Washington: AEC, 1972), 65, 172, 408–9, 548; Richard Rhodes, *Dark Sun: The Making of the Hydrogen Bomb* (New York: Simon & Schuster, 1995), 379.

28 'McCormack, new vice-president, is a man of great distinction,' *The Tech* 77, no. 29, 4 October 1957, 1; Jon Wigert, 'Profile: General Mac,' *The Tech* 78, no. 36, 21 October 1958, 2; Mike McNutt, 'Vice-president resigns: McCormack to head Comsat,' *The Tech* 85, no. 20, 20 October 1965, 1; Lily Kay, *Who Wrote the Book of Life? A History of the Genetic Code* (Stanford, CA: Stanford University Press, 2000), 300–2.

29 Robert Meisel and John Jacobs, *MITRE: The First Twenty Years, A History of the MITRE Corporation (1958–1978)* (Bedford, MA: MITRE Corp., 1979), 16–8, 114–5, 121; Samuel Jay Keyser, 'Our manner of speaking,' *Technology Review*, February 1964, 20; Arnold Zwicky, Joyce Friedman, Barbara Hall (Partee) and Donald Walker, 'The MITRE syntactic analysis procedure for transformational grammars,' *AFIPS Conference Proceedings: Fall Joint Computer Conference* (1965), 317.

30 Arnold Zwicky, 'Grammars of number theory: Some examples,' Working Paper W-6671 (Bedford, MA: The MITRE Corporation, 1963), foreword, back page, https://web.stanford.edu/~zwicky/grammar-of-number-theory.pdf (accessed February 2018); Arnold Zwicky and Stephen Isard, 'Some aspects of tree theory,' Working Paper W-6674 (Bedford, MA: The MITRE Corporation, 1963), foreword, back page, https://web.stanford.edu/~zwicky/some-aspects-of-tree-theory.pdf (accessed February 2018).

31 Chris Knight, 'Chomsky's students recall their time at the MITRE Corporation,' February 2018, http://scienceandrevolution.org/blog/2018/2/17/chomskys-students-recall-their-time-at-the-mitre-corporation (accessed May 2018).

    Another MIT researcher, Lieutenant Jay Keyser, further clarified the military relevance of Chomskyan linguistics when, in a 1965 article, he suggested that the computer languages then being used in various command and control systems could be replaced with an 'English control language' based on Chomsky's theories. Keyser illustrated his article with words such as 'aircraft' and 'missile' and sample sentences such as: 'The bomber the fighter attacked landed safely.' Samuel Jay Keyser, 'Linguistic theory and system design,' in *Information System Sciences*, eds Joseph Spiegel and Donald Walker (Washington, DC: MITRE Corp., 1965), 495–505.

32 Anthony Debons, 'Command and control: Technology and social impact,' *Advances in Computers*, 11 (1971), 354.

33 Bert Green, Carol Chomsky, Kenneth Laughery and Alice Wolf, *The Baseball Program: An Automatic Question-Answerer, Vol. 1* (Bedford, MA: MIT Lincoln Laboratory, 1963); Bert Green, *Digital Computers in Research: An Introduction for Behavioral and Social Scientists* (New York: McGraw-Hill, 1963), viii, 238–48, 258.

34 Dan Robinson, 'Profiles in research: Interview with Bert F. Green,' *Journal of Educational and Behavioral Statistics* 29, no. 2 (Summer 2004), 262–3.

35 Chris Knight, 'Chomsky's students recall their time at the MITRE Corporation,' 18 February 2018, http://scienceandrevolution.org/blog/2018/2/17/chomskys-students-recall-their-time-at-the-mitre-corporation (accessed May 2018).

36 Noam Chomsky, 'Day at night: Noam Chomsky, author, lecturer, philosopher, and linguist,' interview by James Day, CUNY TV, 9 April 1974, 23 mins. https://www.youtube.com/watch?v=rH8SicnqSC4.

37 Ron Chepesiuk, *Sixties Radicals, Then and Now: Candid Conversations with those who Shaped the Era* (Jefferson, NC: McFarland, 1995), 138–9.

38 Noam Chomsky and James Peck, ed. *The Chomsky Reader* (London: Serpent's Tail, 1988), 54–5.

39 Howard Friel, *Chomsky and Dershowitz: On endless war and the end of civil liberties* (Northampton, MA: Interlink Books, 2013), ch. 2. 'Course 21 offers two new subjects,' *The Tech* 85, no. 17, 29 September 1965, 1; 'Committee to meet, plan participation in Viet Nam protests,' *The Tech* 85, no. 17, 29 September 1965, 11; Ted Nygreen, 'Vietnam demonstrations, students join protests,' *The Tech* 85, no. 20, 20 October 1965, 1; Chomsky, *Class Warfare* (1996), 100.

40 Chomsky in *The Chomsky Reader* (1988), 55.

41 Konrad Koerner and Matsuji Tajima, *Noam Chomsky: A Personal Bibliography, 1951–1986* (Amsterdam/Philadelphia: John Benjamins, 1986), 91; Robert Barsky, *Noam Chomsky: A Life of Dissent* (Cambridge, MA: MIT Press, 1997), 16.

42 Noam Chomsky, *Radical Priorities*, ed. Carlos P. Otero (Oakland: AK Press, 2003), 175.

43 'The responsibility of intellectuals' in Chomsky, *American Power and the New Mandarins* (1969), 323.

44 Chomsky, *American Power and the New Mandarins* (1969), 7.

45 For more on the extreme abstraction of Chomsky's linguistics, see Chris Knight, *Decoding Chomsky* (2018), chs. 15 and 16.

46 Barsky, *Noam Chomsky* (1997), 140.

47 Milan Rai, *Chomsky's Politics* (London and New York: Verso, 1995), 131. In this quote, Chomsky is clearly referring to Walt Rostow, whose right to return to work at MIT he openly defended in 1969. Barsky, *Noam Chomsky* (1997), 141.

48 Chomsky in *Language and Politics*, ed. Otero (1988), 419.
49 Chomsky in *Language and Politics*, ed. Otero (1988), 419.
50 Barsky, *Noam Chomsky* (1997), 141.
51 Noam Chomsky, '"The Responsibility of Intellectuals": An exchange,' *New York Review of Books*, 23 March 1967.
52 Noam Chomsky, 'Reply to critics,' *New York Review of Books*, 20 April 1967.
53 'Chomsky accepts post; Ward Professor named,' *The Tech* 86, no. 20, 22 April 1966, 1; Noam Chomsky, 'Noam Chomsky – The war on unions and workers' rights' (1995), 2 hours 2–5 mins, https://www.youtube.com/watch?v=lhgaARgTdAk (accessed March 2018).
54 William Thompson, *At the Edge of History* (New York: Harper and Row, 1971), 62, 67.

6
The abdication of responsibility

Craig Murray

Chomsky sets out a hard test at the end of his essay. He quotes Dwight Macdonald: 'Only those who are willing to resist authority themselves when it conflicts too intolerably with their personal moral code, only they have the right to condemn the death-camp paymaster.'

I intend, as myself a whistleblower who paid the price with his career and livelihood, to claim that right. I take this as licence to be freely condemnatory in what follows!

Some historical perspective

After a brief period in the 1960s and 1970s when progress appeared to be made in western societies in personal freedoms, in social mobility and reduction of wealth inequality, things have now regressed. In the 1970s it was still possible to subscribe in essence to the Whig historical theory of progress, and indeed I did so.

We now live in darkened times. The surveillance state has become all pervasive. Obama's persecution of whistleblowers should give pause to the many who seem to think intolerance was invented by Trump. The imperialist projection of American power has widened in scope and ambition since Chomsky wrote.

It is worth noting the clear-eyed recognition in Chomsky's work that the Soviet Union was also a rival empire. Even while deploring irrational Russophobia and the continual threat posture of encirclement – which Chomsky also notes in his essay – I always find it is worth reminding people that Russia itself still is an empire. Much of its current land – and I mean Russia itself, not the former Soviet Republics – was acquired in the nineteenth century by imperial conquest precisely contemporary with British acquisitions in India or indeed the westward expansion of the USA. These territories are majority Muslim. Russian imperialism is quite real.

Academic freedom

Chomsky's essay refers to academics with influence in the public sphere, and I suspect in general that influence has reduced. But we must also mark that the scope of academic freedom has declined significantly in the last few decades.

Universities are now expected to function as corporations. The bottom line has become all important, and the notion of a democratic self-governing community has vanished after an onslaught of macho corporate governance culture, including the ludicrously high levels of remuneration for executives such a culture involves. Furthermore, the value of universities is frequently defined by government in terms of the commercially viable knowledge it can pass to the corporate sector, or the well-conditioned corporate labour it can churn out. Tenure is shrinking. Funding has become short term and dependent on continual measurement of research outputs, putting the funders in de facto academic and intellectual control.

I am afraid I suspect that junior faculty today organising teach-ins like those of 1967 to which Chomsky refers would have their careers substantially damaged. Indeed, I suspect a young Chomsky would be instructed to give up other interests and devote himself solely to a narrow definition of linguistics.

Public intellectuals

As a historian I enjoyed Chomsky's castigation of some of that profession. It caused me to reflect on the 'historians' whose views on public policy are sought in the UK and who are called up by the media as commentators: Andrew Roberts, David Starkey, Niall Ferguson. All are on any analysis well to the right of the political spectrum. Ferguson has made a career of or regurgitating the nonsense which Chomsky derided in his essay.

Indeed, it is impossible now to imagine that the public intellectuals the BBC admired 50 years ago, such as Bertrand Russell and AJP Taylor, would ever be given significant air time now. Support for nuclear disarmament or the nationalisation of major industries would put them way beyond the window of permitted thought. The vicious media assault upon Jeremy Corbyn shows the reaction to even the mildest radicalism.

The media and the narrowing of political thought

This process of the narrowing of permitted political thought has taken place over the long term. In 1879, Gladstone – campaigning in an election that brought him to power for his second term as Prime Minister – stated in a major speech that Afghans fighting British troops were justified in doing so because Britain had invaded their country: 'If they resisted, would not you have done the same'? Gladstone asked.[1] It is a simple moral test. But who can doubt that in the UK or the US today, to say that anybody fighting 'our' troops might be justified would bring a unanimous hellstorm of media condemnation combining false patriotism with militarism?

Still less is there interest in the media in exposing the truth and holding the government to account. In the UK recently, the Attorney General gave a speech in defence of the UK's drone policy, the assassination of people – including British nationals – abroad. This execution without a hearing is based on several criteria, he reassured us. His speech was repeated slavishly in the British media. In fact, the *Guardian* newspaper simply republished the government press release absolutely verbatim, and stuck a reporter's byline at the top.[2]

The media have no interest in a critical appraisal of the process by which the British government regularly executes without trial. Yet in fact it is extremely interesting. The genesis of the policy lay in the appointment of Daniel Bethlehem as the Foreign and Commonwealth Office's Chief Legal Adviser. Jack Straw made the appointment, and for the first time ever it was external, and not from the Foreign Office's own large team of world-renowned international lawyers. The reason for that is not in dispute. Every single one of the FCO's legal advisers had advised that the invasion of Iraq was illegal, and Straw wished to find a new head of the department more in tune with the neo-conservative world view.

Straw went to extremes. He appointed Daniel Bethlehem, the lawyer who provided the legal advice to Benjamin Netanyahu on the 'legality' of building the great wall hemming in the Palestinians away from their land and water resources.

Bethlehem provided an opinion on the legality of drone strikes which is, to say the least, controversial. To give one example, Bethlehem accepts that established principles of international law dictate that lethal force may be used only to prevent an attack which is 'imminent'. Bethlehem argues that for an attack to be 'imminent' does not require it to be 'soon'. Indeed you can kill to avert an 'imminent attack' even if you have no information on when and where it will be. You can instead rely on your target's 'pattern of behaviour'; that is, if he has attacked before, it is reasonable to assume he will attack again and that such an attack is 'imminent'.[3]

There is a much deeper problem: that the evidence against the target is often extremely dubious. Yet even allowing the evidence to be perfect, it is beyond me that the state can kill in such circumstances without it being considered a death penalty imposed without trial for past crimes, rather than to frustrate another 'imminent' one.

You would think that background would make an interesting story. Yet the entire 'serious' British media published the government line, without a single journalist, not one, writing about the fact that Bethlehem's proposed definition of 'imminent' has been widely rejected by the international law community. The public knows none of this. They just 'know' that drone strikes are keeping us safe from deadly attack by terrorists, because the government says so, and nobody has attempted to give them other information.

I think we can say, 50 years on, that as a general rule, the responsibility of intellectuals to tell the truth has been well and truly abdicated. More than ever is truth telling at odds with career prospects, and most 'intellectuals' care a great deal more about their careers than about the truth.

Notes

1   Speech given in Dalkeith on 26 November 1879. Paul Adelman, *Gladstone, Disraeli and Later Victorian Politics* (Harlow: Longman, 1970), 90.
2   Owen Boycott. 'Attorney general calls for new legal basis for pre-emptive military strikes.' *The Guardian*, 11 January 2017.
3   Daniel Bethlehem, 'Principles relevant to the scope of a state's right to self-defense against an imminent or actual armed attack by non-state actor,' *American Journal of International Law* 106 (2012).

7
Replies and commentary

Noam Chomsky

Commentary on Walker

Jackie Walker's eloquent call for intellectual activism raises fundamental questions about the very concept of 'the intellectual', which, she argues persuasively, 'needs fundamental rethinking'. She is quite right to observe that the concept has been constructed to exclude those 'divorced from the structures of power, carrying the stigma of historical oppression.' Why should the concept exclude Peter Tosh and his message of liberation in song and dance 'directed to the mass of the people ... formulated in a genre that can be heard by any who choose to hear and take up its rhythms'? Why exclude 'the intellectuals of our movement, the mothers and fathers, cooks and cleaners, the unemployed, fast-food workers, the office workers – all are our intellectuals, all who resist while standing witness to the truth'? Or to refer to the discussion at the UCL conference (p. 108), why exclude 'Native Americans, black activists and others [who] have always been quite prominent in trying to break through these ugly and disgraceful misinterpretations'?

The concept of 'intellectual' is indeed a curious one. A Nobel laureate in physics who keeps to exploring the mysteries of quantum mechanics is not called an intellectual, nor is the janitor who cleans the labs and offices, who may have sharp insights into the nature of the society and deep understanding of it, as well as valuable ideas as to how to overcome the social pathologies to which Walker rightly directs our attention.

In common usage, as discussed at the conference (p. 119), the term 'intellectual' is generally reserved for those with a degree of privilege who use their opportunities to become involved in the public arena. But that is a usage that merits challenge, as Walker discusses.

Commentary on Smith and Smith

Restricting ourselves nevertheless to the common usage, let's turn to the concept of 'responsibility of intellectuals' (RI). We see at once that it is ambiguous: there are distinct groups of intellectuals who see themselves as having very different responsibilities.

A useful distinction, which captures essential issues, is put forth by Neil and Amahl Smith in their 'reflections'. They quote my 'sardonic description' of two categories of intellectuals: the '"technocratic and policy-oriented intellectuals" (the "good guys", in the eyes of the establishment, who merely serve external power) and the "value-oriented intellectuals" (the "bad guys" … who engage in critical analysis and "delegitimation")'.

My description was indeed sardonic, but I cannot claim originality for the characterisation of the two categories of intellectuals, which in the original was anything but sardonic. It was dead serious, a fact of no slight importance and with considerable bearing on RI. I was quoting from a revealing document, the first – and I think most significant – publication of the Trilateral Commission, *The Crisis of Democracy*.[1] The Commission consisted largely of liberal internationalists from the three centres of capitalist democracy: the US, Europe and Japan. Its general political orientation is illustrated by the fact that almost the entirety of the Carter administration – indeed Carter himself – was drawn from its ranks.

The report of the Commission praises the 'technocratic and policy-oriented intellectuals' as serious and honourable, fulfilling their responsibilities to design and implement policy soberly and responsibly (one concept of RI). It sharply criticises the 'value-oriented intellectuals' who see their responsibility differently. In the eyes of the Commission, such intellectuals are sentimental and emotional (or with more insidious designs). They promote disorder and corrupt the youth, helping bring about the 'crisis of democracy'.

The concept of 'technocratic and policy-oriented intellectuals' was captured succinctly by Henry Kissinger at the time when he was angling for a position in the incoming administration. One qualifies as an 'expert', Kissinger explained, by 'elaborating and defining' the consensus of one's constituency 'at a high level'. In short: providing expert services to the powerful.[2]

The 'crisis of democracy' that concerned the Trilateral intellectuals was the 'excessive democracy' that disfigured the 1960s, 'the time of troubles', as it is often called – or, from a different point of view, the time when the country was considerably civilised. The crisis was brought about when normally passive parts of the population – the young, the old, women, minorities, workers, farmers and those from other such sectors – sought to enter the political arena to advocate for their interests, imposing too much of a burden on the state and rendering the country ungovernable. Rejecting the common idea that the cure for democracy's ills is more democracy, the Trilateral intellectuals called for more 'moderation in democracy', a return to passivity and conformity. The American rapporteur Samuel Huntington, Harvard Professor of the Science of Government, recalled earlier years when 'Truman had been able to govern the country with the cooperation of a relatively small number of Wall Street lawyers and bankers', so that democracy functioned smoothly, with no unsupportable burden on the state, and no crisis.

In passing we should note that there was nothing new about the Trilateralist concern over the insubordination of the 'ignorant and meddlesome outsiders', the general public, which must be 'put in its place' so that the 'responsible men' may 'live free of the trampling and the roar of a bewildered herd' as they conduct affairs of state responsibly, to borrow the words of America's leading twentieth-century liberal intellectual, Walter Lippmann, in what his editors call a 'political philosophy for liberal democracy'. Such fears can be traced back to the earliest modern democratic revolution in seventeenth-century England, when the 'giddy multitude of beasts in men's shapes', as they were called by the self-described 'men of best quality', rejected the basic framework of the civil conflict raging in England between king and parliament, and called for government 'by countrymen like ourselves, that know our wants', not by 'knights and gentlemen that make us laws, that are chosen for fear and do but oppress us, and do not know the people's sores'.[3] The concern of the men of best quality has not abated since.

As I mentioned, the Trilateral Commission concerns are voiced from the liberal end of the mainstream spectrum. At about the same time, a counterpart appears from the opposite end, the 'Powell memorandum' sent by corporate lobbyist (later Supreme Court Justice) Lewis Powell to the Chamber of Commerce, the major business association.[4] Powell too perceived a crisis, one of utmost severity. His memorandum called upon the business community to rise up to defend itself against the assault on freedom led by Ralph Nader, Herbert Marcuse and other miscreants who had taken over the universities, the media and the government and were destroying the foundations of our free society. The rhetoric is as interesting as the contents, reflecting the perceptions of Powell's audience, desperate about the slight diminution in their overwhelming power – rather like a spoiled three-year-old who has a piece of candy taken away. The memorandum was influential in circles that matter for policy formation.

Returning to the liberal concerns, the Commission warned that the 'value-oriented intellectuals' contribute to the crisis by 'devot[ing] themselves to the derogation of leadership, the challenging of authority, and the unmasking and delegitimation of established institutions'. Particularly dangerous is their role in undermining the institutions responsible for 'the indoctrination of the young' – schools, universities, churches. They also infected the media, which, under their baleful influence, had become so extreme in their attacks on good order that the government might have to intervene to curb their excesses, the Trilateralists warned.

While the absurdity of the picture does not approach that of the Powell Memorandum, at the core it reflects the same fears that the 'bewildered herd' might be chipping away at the edifice of elite control.

At the height of the 'time of troubles', in 1968, the Kennedy–Johnson National Security adviser and former Harvard Dean McGeorge Bundy went even beyond the Commission in condemning the value-oriented intellectuals. They are 'wild men in the wings', who not only criticise the judgements and actions of our leaders, but even question their motives! And still worse, one might add, they do so by citing their own pronouncements in internal documents and reporting the actions that conform to them. The style of the charges carries us back to the earliest use of the term 'intellectual' in the modern sense, at the time of the Dreyfus trial (p. 102). Plus ça change ...

These familiar charges bring to mind another term which, like the concept 'intellectual', has a curious modern usage: the term 'dissident intellectual'. Overwhelmingly it has been used to refer to dissidents in Russia and its domains, virtually never to refer to those in the US and Latin America. A look at the rather odd collection of 'dissidents' in Wikipedia (including Hitler, David Duke – and me) gives a general sense: overwhelmingly Russian. In light of both fact and elementary principle, that usage is of some interest.

As for facts, from 1960 to

the Soviet collapse in 1990, the numbers of political prisoners, torture victims, and executions of non-violent political dissenters in Latin America vastly exceeded those in the Soviet Union and its East European satellites. In other words, from 1960 to 1990, the

Soviet bloc as a whole was less repressive, measured in terms of human victims, than many individual Latin American countries[5]

– a toll that included many religious martyrs, and mass slaughter as well, consistently supported or even initiated in Washington.

Nevertheless, the victims in US domains are not 'dissidents', not even the six prominent Latin American intellectuals, Jesuit priests, murdered in November 1989 by the elite Atlacatl brigade of the Salvadoran army, fresh from renewed US training and acting on the explicit orders of the high command, which was never distant from the American embassy.[6]

In the US the incident is scarcely known, though outside of western intellectual circles such matters are readily understood, of course in the countries directly targeted by US-backed state terrorism. Thus the journal *Proceso* of the Jesuit university in El Salvador observed:

> If Lech Walesa had been doing his organising work in El Salvador, he would have already entered into the ranks of the disappeared – at the hands of 'heavily armed men dressed in civilian clothes'; or have been blown to pieces in a dynamite attack on his union headquarters. If Alexander Dubček were a politician in our country, he would have been assassinated like Héctor Oquelí [the social democratic leader assassinated in Guatemala, apparently by Salvadoran death squads]. If Andrei Sakharov had worked here in favor of human rights, he would have met the same fate as Herbert Anaya [one of the many murdered leaders of the independent Salvadoran Human Rights Commission CDHES]. If Ota-Sik or Vaclav Havel had been carrying out their intellectual work in El Salvador, they would have wound up one sinister morning, lying on the patio of a university campus with their heads destroyed by the bullets of an elite army battalion.[7]

Moving from fact to principle, what should be the operative principle is clear enough: our prime concern should be the crimes for which we share responsibility and that we can do something about, that we can mitigate or terminate. We understand this truism well enough in the case of official enemies. It was of little moment what intellectuals in the USSR said about US domains, but we care a great deal about what they said about Russia. We honour the Russian dissidents who lay bare the faults of their own societies, and dismiss, with contempt, the apparatchiks who repeat patriotic pieties.

At home, the judgements and values are reversed. Those who assure us that US intents are benign, however mistaken, are the 'responsible men', while those who question the pieties are 'wild men in the wings' who can be ignored or ridiculed. As the acerbic American commentator HL Mencken once wrote, referring to an Irish-American writer who was in and out of jail on trivial charges, 'If [he] were a Russian, read in translation, all the professors would be hymning him'.[8]

Such distinctions often come to the fore with considerable clarity. One such moment was the end of the Vietnam War in 1975. Putting aside the wild men in the wings, reactions were roughly divided between hawks and doves. The former argued that with determination we could have won, sometimes adding 'stab-in-the-back' recriminations. The doves, at the extreme end, held that:

> The early American decisions on Indochina can be regarded as blundering efforts to do good. But by 1969 it was clear to most of the world – and most Americans – that the intervention had been a disastrous mistake … The argument [against the war] was that the United States had misunderstood the cultural and political forces at work in Indochina – that it was in a position where it could not impose a solution except at a price too costly to itself.[9]

There was also a different view, but it did not enter the debate: that the war was 'fundamentally wrong and immoral', not 'a mistake'. Though that position didn't make it into the mainstream hawk–dove debate, it was in fact held: namely, by a large majority of the public, as was found in the investigations of the Chicago Council on Foreign Relations, which conducts regular studies of popular attitudes on a wide range of issues. The figures held steady until 1999, after which it seems that the question was dropped. These are quite astonishing figures for an open question, particularly when respondents are drawing the conclusion in virtual isolation, the conception being inexpressible and unthinkable in mainstream discussion. One can only guess what the figures would be if the rigid doctrinal framework were penetrable.

There are, of course, questions about just what people meant when they took this position. Reviewing the data of two decades in 1999, the director of the studies, political scientist John Rielly, concludes that the responses show a 'preference to avoid undertaking major burdens in foreign interventions'. Possibly. Or possibly they show that the public agrees with the wild men in the wings. It wouldn't have been hard to determine the answer, but apparently the inquiry was never undertaken. Similar questions arise about a great many issues, a matter that merits much more attention than it receives.

Commentary on Allott

These considerations bring us to some serious questions raised by Nicholas Allott about the validity of the apparent RI truism that intellectuals should seek to speak the truth. Allott raises two issues: (1) doing so may be irrelevant to voters, because 'There is strong evidence that voting is not primarily driven by evaluation of the policies on offer ... The challenge to RI from this research is that telling the truth and exposing lies may not make much difference'; (2) telling the truth may be counterproductive because of the 'backfire effect'; doing so may simply reinforce refuted beliefs in reaction.

Allott provides reasons why the RI truism should withstand these objections. On (2) he writes that the idea that the effect is 'always operative and dominant ... cannot be right. People do change their minds, and at least some of the time when they do so it is because they have been persuaded by evidence against their prior belief.' On (1), he quotes my comment that 'Being alone, you can't do anything – But if you join with other people you can make changes', and he observes that 'deepening democracy so that it more closely matches the popular ideal will require considerable changes to education, the media and the democratic system itself'. Both observations seem to me to point in the right direction.

On people changing their minds, that's a common experience in activism. One striking example, discussed earlier, pp. 5–6, is the rapid change in popular attitudes about the Vietnam War from 1965/6 to late 1967. It was not the result of some dramatic new event but rather of several years of education and organisation under difficult circumstances, which finally led to a breakthrough. The change was very dramatic where I was at MIT (pp. 115–6), which was in the forefront in this regard in the northeastern US (and unusual if not unique in the country, particularly with regard to academic participation in war resistance). But it was far more widespread.

There are other cases where it took far longer to break through the barriers of evasion and deceit. One highly significant case, which happened to be a personal obsession of mine for many years, is what is arguably the closest approximation to true genocide in the post-war era, the western-backed Indonesian invasion of East Timor in 1975.[10] Finally, after literally decades of dedicated work on the part of a very few people, mostly young – notably the unsung hero Arnold Kohen – enough public pressure developed for President Clinton to call off the slaughter and open the way for survival and independence, as could have been done from the start. But minds were changed – or more accurately, opened, at least among large parts of the general public if not intellectual elites, which continue, routinely, to ignore or simply deny the facts.[11]

There are many other cases, and they deserve careful scrutiny, because what actually happened – often known primarily to participants – is commonly reshaped to satisfy the needs of power and doctrine.

More generally, the two challenges to RI that Allott discusses appear to have a common root: recognition on the part of the public that they are simply not represented in the political system – as is in fact substantially the case. Careful studies comparing political preferences with decisions of elected representatives show that a large majority of voters are literally disenfranchised: their own representatives disregard their opinions and listen to other voices, those of the concentrated economic powers that substantially determine electoral outcomes by campaign spending, that provide the overwhelming majority of influential lobbyists who often virtually write legislation, and that shape politics in other familiar ways.[12] Furthermore, citizens appear to be quite aware that they are disenfranchised. Allott cites polls that consistently, at least since the Reagan years, show that – often by overwhelming majorities – the public believe that 'the government is pretty much run by a few big interests looking out for themselves', contrary to endless propaganda in media and journals of opinion, schools and universities.

People do not have to read academic political science to know that their preferences are ignored on a wide range of issues on which extensive polling shows sharp divergence of public opinion from policy, and to realise that 'I don't vote because my vote don't count anyway', thanks to radical gerrymandering and voter suppression measures, honed to a high art by the Republican party (not without predecessors) and supported by the most reactionary Supreme Court in living memory.[13]

The press often helps by suppressing (or even deriding) the facts. For example, the *Economist* assures us that the 'grim, mirthless' Bernie Sanders with his 'crotchety-great-uncle charisma' is an 'indulgence' that Democrats can 'ill afford', and that fortunately, silly season 'has probably passed'. After all, we are instructed, his main ideas 'have little support within [the Democratic] party, let alone America': only the support of 75 per cent of Democrats, 59 per cent of the general public (national health care, 'Medicare-for-all') and of 80 per cent of Clinton voters, 45 per cent of Trump voters (tuition-free college). Facts that readers are spared.[14]

To cite one of many examples from US media, striking though less egregious, polls on taxes over 40 years show that the public consistently wants lower taxes for themselves and higher taxes on business and the wealthy. The former result is reported regularly, not the latter. Policy moves in the opposite direction, to a ridiculous extreme under the Trump tax scam.[15]

During the neoliberal period, policies have been designed and implemented that predictably lead to the sharp concentration of wealth while the majority of the public face stagnation or decline, in the US continuing to the time of writing (August 2018) – facts that are not entirely suppressed. Thus an upbeat lead story in the *New York Times* lauding the amazing successes of the economy does inform the reader, in paragraph 31 of the continuation page, that real wages continue their decline.[16]

By a natural and familiar process, concentration of wealth leads to increased concentration of political power and increased marginalisation of the public.[17] This is in accord with the guiding principle enunciated by Margaret Thatcher: 'there is no such thing as society'. We should not turn to government to solve our problems; rather, each of us must 'take responsibility for ourselves' and individually help 'those who are unfortunate'.[18]

Unwittingly no doubt, Thatcher was paraphrasing Marx's bitter condemnation of the autocratic governments that sought to turn society into a 'sack of potatoes': isolated individuals, lacking organisation and supportive institutions. They must then face the problems of life on their own – and in the neoliberal period, with 'growing worker insecurity' in 'flexible labor markets' – Alan Greenspan's explanation for the health of the economy he was running while he was still lauded as 'St Alan', before the 2007 crash.

A sack of potatoes can be expected to yield the kind of results found in the studies that Allott cites, though it would likely be quite different in periods when militant labour activism and flourishing popular movements have been able to influence political choices, not simply to observe in mounting disillusionment.

The happy days when private power can rampage freely may not last too long, however. Much to the consternation of elite opinion, the sack of potatoes has not settled into passivity, in the US or elsewhere. The *Economist* does recognise unhappily that the 'grim, mirthless' Bernie Sanders is the most popular political figure in the country. And despite efforts to keep him in the shadows, the popular movement he organised is far from having 'berned out', the fond hope of the *Economist* editors. It is active and growing, along with others.

It's also worth remembering that the most remarkable fact about the 2016 election was not the election of a billionaire with huge financial and media support. Rather, it was the Sanders campaign, which broke with over a century of elections in which outcomes are predictable with remarkable accuracy, both for president and Congress, from the single variable of campaign spending. That could turn out to be a significant turning point in American politics, just as the Corbyn movement might be in England and DiEM25 and others on the continent. The growing popular bitterness about the consequences of the neoliberal assault of the past generation can bring forth ugly reactions, as we see everywhere, but there are positive signs as well.

Antonio Gramsci's comment from his prison cell is once again all too apt: 'The crisis consists precisely in the fact that the old is dying and the new cannot be born; in this interregnum a great variety of morbid symptoms appear' – but hopeful signs as well.

Commentary on Rai

Also all too apt, regrettably, is Milan Rai's harrowing review of how Britain has used nuclear weapons, along with his explanation of the real meaning of deterrence and his analysis of how media coverage, while providing information, has framed the issues in ways that implicitly entrench doctrines of the propaganda system that distort reality.[19] Daniel Ellsberg's observation about the regular use of nuclear weapons, which Rai quotes, is entirely accurate. In his recent book *Doomsday Machine* – essential reading – Ellsberg identifies no fewer than 25 occasions when the US has employed nuclear weapons in the manner that Rai reviews.[20]

It is quite important to add the little-known fact that Ellsberg's observation is, in fact, official US policy, outlined in a very important document that has not received the attention it deserves: a Clinton-era study by the US Strategic Command (STRATCOM), which controls nuclear weapons command and control, military operations in space, missile defence and related matters.[21] The central conclusion of the STRATCOM study is that the reliance on nuclear weapons is to remain fundamentally unchanged after the end of the Cold War, except that the scope of potential targets extends beyond Cold War enemies to 'rogue' states – in practice, those that are disobedient. Adopting Ellsberg's principle, the document states that 'Although we are not likely [sic] to use nuclear weapons in less than matters of the greatest national importance, or in less than extreme circumstances, nuclear weapons always cast a shadow over any crisis or conflict'. And, in this sense, are constantly used.

Extending the principle, STRATCOM stresses the need for *credibility*: Washington's strategy must be 'convincing [and] immediately discernible'. The US should have available 'the full range of responses', but nuclear weapons are the most important of these, because 'Unlike chemical or biological weapons, the extreme destruction from a nuclear explosion is immediate, with few if any palliatives to reduce its effect'.

One section, headed: 'Maintaining Ambiguity', explains that it is important that 'planners should not be too rational about determining … what the opponent values the most', all of which must be targeted. Furthermore, 'it hurts to portray ourselves as too fully rational and cool-headed … That the US may become irrational and vindictive if its vital interests are attacked should be a part of the national persona we project'. It is 'beneficial' for our strategic posture if 'some elements may appear to be potentially "out of control"' – chilling words at any time, but particularly in Trumpland.

Note that the document establishes the 'madman theory' that was attributed to Richard Nixon in a memoir by his chief of staff, HR Haldeman, and bitterly condemned. Under Clinton, however, it was formulated as official doctrine.

Nuclear weapons 'seem destined to be the centerpiece of US strategic deterrence for the foreseeable future', the STRATCOM report concludes. We should therefore reject a 'no first use policy', even against non-nuclear states, and should make it clear to adversaries that our 'reaction' may 'either be response or preemptive', hence in violation of the UN Charter, the 'supreme law of the land' under the US Constitution, were anyone to care. Also dismissed is the Non-Proliferation Treaty, except when it can be used as a pretext for threatening, perhaps attacking, official enemies.

Occasionally the same prevailing doctrine breaks through the general silence, though not to the general public, or even the scholarly community, with rare exceptions. Thus Carter's Defense Secretary Harold Brown called on Congress to fund strategic nuclear capabilities because with them, 'our other forces become meaningful instruments of military and political power'.[22] This is the STRATCOM principle enunciated in *Essentials*.

Possibly in reaction to this document, the former head of STRATCOM, General Lee Butler, wrote that throughout his long professional military career he had been 'among the most avid of these keepers of the faith in nuclear weapons', but felt that in his judgement 'they served us extremely ill', for reasons he outlines. He asks

> By what authority do succeeding generations of leaders in the nuclear-weapons states usurp the power to dictate the odds

of continued life on our planet? Most urgently, why does such breathtaking audacity persist at a moment when we should stand trembling in the face of our folly and united in our commitment to abolish its most deadly manifestations?[23]

A good question.

A review of the record provides ample support for General Butler's plea for sanity. The record reveals that it is a near miracle that humans have survived the nuclear age. Repeatedly, terminal disaster has come very close, usually by accident (equipment failure and the like), sometimes by reckless acts of leaders. And we can hardly have faith that miracles will persist.

In 1947, at the dawn of the nuclear age, the *Bulletin of Atomic Scientists* established its Doomsday Clock. Each year, scientists and political analysts set the minute hand a certain distance from midnight: terminal disaster. In 1947 it was set at 7 minutes to midnight, halcyon days by our standards. Over the years it has oscillated, depending on world circumstances. Once, in 1953, it reached 2 minutes to midnight after the US and then the USSR exploded thermonuclear weapons, revealing that human intelligence had gained the capacity to destroy everything. In 2016, the hand was moved to 3 minutes to midnight, now taking into account failure to deal with global warming. When Trump took office, it was moved forward to 2½ minutes to midnight, and a year later, moved again to 2 minutes to midnight, as close as it has been to the end during the nuclear age. Not attractive prospects, unless the nuclear powers can come to their senses.

Commentary on Murray

Craig Murray's sober reflections on the current scene also do not offer attractive prospects. They are particularly compelling in the light of his deep knowledge and personal experience, including his courageous exposure of awful atrocities in Uzbekistan, which infuriated the British Foreign Office and the US embassy (the exposures, that is, not the atrocities) and cost him his diplomatic career, propelling him to a life of activism. Again, his reflections are reminiscent of Gramsci's observations from Mussolini's prison cells on the current scene of his day.

The 'morbid symptoms' are surely real enough, but I still feel that the prospects are not as grim as his portrayal suggests: in part, because I think his account underestimates the civilising effect of the activism of the 60s – the famous 'time of troubles' in elite perception – and its consequences to the present.

One illustration is opposition to aggression. In remarks earlier (pp. 5–6), I described briefly the context in which my 1966 talk on RI was given at Harvard, in one of the outposts of liberalism and higher education in the US. It took many years of intense effort, briefly mentioned above (pp. 5–6) – talks, meetings, demonstrations, protests, resistance – to bring about the great changes in popular consciousness that finally took place by late 1967, when major protests erupted against the US wars in Indochina. I might have added that by then South Vietnam, the main target of the attacks, was utterly devastated. In 1967 the highly respected and bitterly anti-Communist military historian and Indochina specialist Bernard Fall warned that 'Vietnam as a cultural and historic entity … is threatened with extinction … [as] the countryside literally dies under the blows of the largest military machine ever unleashed on an area of this size', referring primarily to South Vietnam where attacks were uninhibited by concerns about international reaction. That was the state of the victims when the tide of public opinion began to turn significantly.

Let's move on to the Reagan administration, which came into office in 1981. Its highest international priority was to escalate the US wars in Central America. The process began by duplicating closely Kennedy's steps 20 years earlier when he escalated the Vietnam War: a White Paper denouncing Communist crimes, a major propaganda campaign about international terrorism directed by the standard enemies, etc. The popular reaction was immediate. The White Paper was quickly exposed as a fraud and there were major protests – right away, not six years later. Reagan backed off and instead launched a campaign of international terrorism throughout the region, relying on clandestine operations and a network of compliant states to support local state terror: Taiwan, Israel, Argentine neo-Nazis (until the overthrow of the military junta in 1983). The consequences were horrendous enough, but nothing like the saturation bombing of heavily populated areas by B-52s, massive chemical warfare and the other atrocities of Vietnam, then all of Indochina.

There is more, of considerable importance. For the first time in history, to my knowledge, citizens of the aggressor not only protested the crimes, but went to live with the victims, often in endangered areas, both to lend assistance and to provide whatever protection is afforded by a white face. In substantial numbers. No one ever thought of going to live in a Vietnamese village. They were coming mostly from middle America, often church groups. I well remember giving talks and attending meetings in the rural south and midwest where people had intimate knowledge of Central America from direct experience, their own and friends and families. And many stayed on. Unsung, of course. But quite real.

Fast forward to 2003, when the US and UK invaded Iraq, the worst crime of this century. For the first time in history, there were huge protests against imperial aggression even before the attack was officially launched. Again, the consequences have been horrendous, but nothing like what they would have been had the aggressors been free to use Vietnam tactics for years. Contrary to common claims, the protests were a success, limited and bitter but real.

The differences over the years reflect the growing awareness and opposition to imperial aggression and terror, one of many significant changes in western culture since the 1960s – nowhere near enough, that much is surely clear, but not insignificant either.

We see the same in other domains. Murray brings up Daniel Bethlehem's 'opinion on the legality of drone strikes which is, to say the least, controversial' – to put it mildly. In the early 1960s, the resort to drone warfare would scarcely have been noticed. Even when Kennedy sent the US Air Force to bomb the South Vietnamese countryside the fact was barely mentioned in the press and protest was undetectable. Speaking personally, the most I was able to do in the early 60s was give talks in someone's living room or a virtually empty church. Efforts to organise public protests in the Boston area (usually at MIT) had to bring together half-a-dozen issues to include Kennedy's escalation in Vietnam.

Today it is very different. There were immediate large-scale protests against the drone assassination programme, including books and even law school articles concluding that the use of combat drones 'appears to fall far short of meeting the international law rules governing resort to armed force and the conduct of armed force'.[24] There was nothing comparable regarding the vastly worse war crimes that threatened 'Vietnam as a cultural and historic entity ... with extinction.'

We might remember as well that as late as the 1960s, the most prominent scholars assured us that when Columbus discovered America (in the terminology of the day), there were only about one million people in the hemisphere, most of which was wild and uncultivated, particularly North America. The figure is off by about 80 million, so it was discovered when the doctrinal walls crumbled. There were advanced civilisations, large cities, sophisticated agricultural projects, extensive commerce – destroyed with particular savagery by British invaders in North America. The perpetrators knew well what they were doing, but it is only recently that their words have reached beyond arcane scholarship. For example, the words of General Henry Knox, the first Secretary of War in the newly liberated American colonies, who described 'the utter extirpation of all the Indians in most populous parts of the Union [by means] more destructive to the Indian natives than the conduct of the conquerors of Mexico and Peru', and warned that 'a future historian may mark the causes of this destruction of the human race in sable colors'. That did begin to happen by the 1970s, thanks to 60s activism. There had been some earlier efforts, notably Helen Hunt Jackson's outstanding study *A Century of Dishonor* (1881), ignored or ridiculed, finally reprinted in 1964 (2,000 copies) as the time of troubles began to gain force, now finally recognised as a classic.

In the 1960s, I doubt that a prominent British historian would have written in the *Times Literary Supplement* that 'it looks almost plausible' that when the facts are in, 'the rulers of the British Empire will ... be perceived to rank with the dictators of the twentieth century as the authors of crimes against humanity on an infamous scale'.[25]

What we were in fact reading at the time, from the liberal extreme of mainstream commentary – the highly regarded liberal columnist of the *New York Times*, James Reston – was that the US was acting in Indochina 'on the principle that military power shall not compel South Vietnam to do what it does not want to do', out of our loyalty to 'the deepest conviction of Western civilization', namely, that 'the individual belongs not to the state but to his Creator' and thus has rights that 'no magistrate or political force may violate'.[26]

This was November 1967, well after the Pentagon demonstrations and the rising resistance movements revealed that anti-war sentiment had gained real traction among the unwashed masses, if not the liberal intellectual elite.

It would be all too easy to continue with the useful exercise of recalling what media commentary was like before the 'time of troubles' had its impact.

The same is true on many other issues. Until the late 1960s, the US had anti-miscegenation laws so severe that the Nazis, searching for precedents, considered US laws but rejected their severity. We may also recall that Britain murdered one of the greatest mathematicians of the century, Alan Turing, also a war hero who helped break German codes, while seeking to cure him of the disease of homosexuality (though he did receive a Royal Pardon for the crime – in 2013). On women's rights, the progress has been radical. Same in many other areas – not enough to be sure, with plenty of challenges ahead, but we should also recognise that dedicated activism has had real effects, and there's no reason to think that those days have ended.

By the 1970s, there was a harsh reaction to the civilising impact of the activism of the 60s – in the eyes of liberal internationalist elites, the 'crisis of democracy' that led to 'the challenging of authority, and the unmasking and delegitimation of established institutions', even those institutions responsible for 'the indoctrination of the young', a dangerous assault led by 'wild men in the wings'. The neoliberal reaction that took off with Reagan and Thatcher has quite definitely contributed to the undermining of academic life that Murray describes, imposing a stultifying business model on universities with a proliferation of administrators and demands for 'commercially viable knowledge it can pass to the corporate sector', a radical increase in tuition fees that has no economic justification, attacks on tenure and all the rest.

All true, but at the same time there has also been liberation from stultifying doctrine, along with quite effective 'unmasking and delegitimation' of what not long ago were virtually sacred dogmas. I don't quite agree with Murray's judgement that faculty today organising 1967-style teach-ins 'would have their careers substantially damaged' (p. 72), at least not because of the substance of their activities and concerns – though they might suffer from the more general maladies of the imposed business models and the shaping of career choices.

And though I understand and sympathise with the perceptions, I'm not persuaded that 'as a general rule, the responsibility of intellectuals to tell the truth has been well and truly abdicated'. It seems to me that horizons have been considerably broadened and that free and independent thought and inquiry have made significant gains, not as a gift from above but, as always, thanks to dedicated efforts – the kind of efforts of which Craig Murray provides an honourable model.

Appendix

I've skipped Chris Knight's contribution, which has no place in a serious discussion of 'RoI', except, perhaps, as an indication of how some intellectuals perceive their responsibility. With considerable distaste, I'll go through some of its highlights.

Knight's essay is another exercise in an intensive campaign he has been waging for several years to establish the thesis that I concocted some exotic form of linguistics, unique in history, to assuage my guilt for my work for the US military machine at 'the heart of the empire' – in his words, my design of approaches to language that are 'so asocial, apolitical and devoid of practical application that I can only assume Chomsky favoured them to keep his conscience clear: he needed them to ensure that his militarily funded linguistics couldn't possibly have any military use'.[27]

As he amplifies here, despite what he sees as Chomsky's 'heartfelt regrets' at not having involved himself in anti-war activities in 1950 or 1955, this tormented creature was

> determined to continue his linguistics research at MIT. But from this point on [1965], he felt morally impelled to clarify that his work was restricted to pure science. His linguistic theories had always been highly abstract but he now needed to stress that if his military sponsors found his models to be unworkable, that did not bother him at all. He would press on with models of language so utterly abstract and ideal – so completely removed from social usage, communication or any kind of technological application – that they were never likely to work for weapons 'command and control' or indeed for any other military purpose. (p. 61)

Let's take this apart step by step. First, just who devoted themselves to work against the Vietnam War in the early 1950s? Answer, essentially no one. My 'heartfelt regrets' were over my failure to depart from the universal norm. And what happened in 1965? Knight knows very well. In 1965 I expanded my anti-war activities from giving talks and organising meetings to direct resistance, initiatives based right at the 'heart of empire', at a time when even in liberal Boston support for the war was so extreme that it was scarcely possible even to organise public events without violent disruption (see pp. 5–6). And I moved very soon on to more direct resistance, as discussed earlier.

So, yes, I was determined to continue my work in a lively and flourishing research environment that also happened to be the main academic centre of anti-war activism. So were the rest of the malefactors in the den of iniquity.

Let's turn then to his main thesis, which he elaborates extensively in the book of his to which he refers: my design of linguistic work 'so asocial, apolitical and devoid of practical application' that Knight 'can only assume' that I undertook it to make sure it could not be used for any military purpose.

For several years, I avoided responding to Knight's charges, but when they appeared (twice) in a widely read journal, I did respond,[28] pointing out that his charges are instantly refuted by the fact that I had been doing this work for years before I had any thought of an appointment at 'the heart of the empire', in fact, as an undergraduate at the University of Pennsylvania in the 1940s and then in graduate work at Harvard in the early 1950s.[29] And that I simply carried the work further after my appointment at MIT in 1955. End of story, at least in a universe where facts matter.

Knight's response to this total refutation of his primary thesis was to evade it and amplify the charges – see note 28 – proceeding to do so again here. He could hardly be more explicit in informing us about the true nature of the campaign he is conducting.

Since that refutation was more than enough, I did not go on to point out what is obvious to anyone with the slightest familiarity with the study of language. But since he amplifies the refuted claim here, perhaps a few words are in order.

The approach that is so 'asocial, apolitical and devoid of practical application' that it must have been devised to avoid exploitation by the US military has been the core of the inquiry into language for millennia, since classical Greece and India, through the medieval Arab and Hebrew grammarians (whom I happened to be studying at U. Penn when I began this work), on to the rich tradition of 'rational and universal grammar' founded in the seventeenth century, including the great achievements of comparative and historical Indo-European grammar, and then twentieth-century structural and anthropological linguistics. And the approach has been adopted without question for very good reasons. It was always understood that the task posed by Aristotle of discovering the relation of sound and meaning poses some of the deepest problems of science and the humanities: to discover the uniquely human capacity to construct in our minds an unbounded array of thoughts that are used in creative and innovative ways, sometimes externalised in sound or some other medium, the core of our cognitive nature, with no analogue elsewhere in the organic world.

These are matters that I discussed extensively from the early 60s at the 'heart of the empire' while studying precedents for contemporary generative grammar, which addresses these tasks directly.[30]

Furthermore, simple logic suffices to show that the traditional concerns, pursued further in the contemporary work that Knight finds incomprehensible, are also the prerequisite for any serious investigation of the social, political and practical applications of language to which he confines his interests. All of this has of course been well understood by the great anthropological linguists, Boas, Sapir and others, as is evident from their linguistic work.

So much for Knight's primary thesis.

In his present amplification of his thesis, Knight focuses on my malevolent contributions to the imperial military machine, so let's have a look at these.

Knight's *pièce de résistance* is my consultantship at the MITRE Corporation, which brought me 'dangerously close to direct collusion with the US military'. MITRE does in fact do military work along with much else; it is, for example, famous for its early work on global warming, brought to high levels of the US government in 1979 by the leader of the project, conscientious objector and Vietnam War protestor Gordon MacDonald.[31] In the early 60s it also had a small language project, where several MIT linguistics students were able to obtain summer jobs. Knight carried out extensive interviews with them in his effort to try to establish my involvement in US militarism, and that of our MIT programme in linguistics more generally. And he is kind enough to cite what he discovered (p. 69, note 31). If we take the trouble to look at the interviews he cites, we instantly discover that they flatly refute all of his claims.

From what he calls 'the most informative' of his interviews, Knight learned that 'Chomsky definitely did come out and consult with us at least once' (since the students were unable to come to my office for their regular appointments), to discuss some technical problems of linguistics (in particular, about adjunction). 'We had total freedom. Everybody could choose their own topic [but] dear Don [the linguist head of the project] realized that he'd have to get us to work collectively on producing a grammar and a parser [that is, standard linguistics, everywhere] in order to convince the generals that it was valuable to hire us ...', though we made it clear that any imaginable military application would be far in the remote future.

Others added that 'I must also say that I never had any whiff of military work at MITRE. Maybe we had to wear badges, I have no recollection of that, but what we talked about had nothing at all to do with command and control or Air Force or anything similar. Our talk was about syntax and confusions about semantics ... I do not recall any time when [Chomsky] was cooperating with the Air Force on anything related to the US war effort anywhere ... From the viewpoint of the grad students who were [at MITRE], it was an interesting and well paid adventure. We were given total freedom' ... We 'had a lot of interesting conversations with Noam. But they were all about linguistics'. Another said that though I never talked politics in my linguistics classes, students did learn about my attitudes (with astonishment, because they were so rare in those days), and he 'became an anti-Vietnam protestor'. At MITRE, he added, it was 'colonels we had to impress, not generals'.

Knight does mention one of these high officers they had to impress, the man he calls 'Colonel Jay Keyser' – in the real world, Lieutenant Samuel Jay Keyser, well known to linguists, who had joined the Reserve Officers Training Corps (ROTC) in 1952, a standard alternative to the draft for students. Knight avoids telling us how the insidious 'Colonel Keyser'[32] was instructing his troops while he was working at MITRE, though he knows the answers from his interviews: Keyser was working 'on Old English metrics' – more accurately on Chaucer, continuing the studies of Middle English for which he is well known in the field.

Keyser told Knight that he could not recall any discussions about 'taking military funding [which was] how the government supported higher education back then'. In fact, as is familiar, in those years US industrial and educational policy was largely funded under the general rubric of 'defence', including the great expansion of institutions of higher education; development of computers, the internet and indeed the basis for most of today's high-tech economy; the national interstate highway system (formally, the 'National System of Interstate and Defense Highways'); and much else. The pretext was so thin that by 1970, when public concern was growing, Congress passed laws limiting military funding to research with some potential relationship to military functions, while still permitting rather lax application.[33]

As much of the public was coming to understand by the late 60s, the process of funding economic development and university expansion under a defence pretext raises many serious questions about functioning democracy, questions that many of us had been raising for years but that are of no interest to Knight, who ignores them completely, even after all of this has been patiently explained to him.

That was my consultancy at MITRE, my main contribution to the military machine, which 'was bringing [me] dangerously close to direct collusion with the US military' – an 'involvement with the MITRE Corporation' to which I never 'made any reference' in my writings. What a strange evasion.

The tale continues. On departing from my (non-existent) consultancy for the military machine at MITRE, Knight reports, I 'became an adviser to MIT's anti-Vietnam War committee, although such activism only ever involved what [Chomsky] calls "a very small group of faculty"', underscoring its insignificance.

Decoding this concoction, the 'very small group of faculty' was not an anti-Vietnam War committee but rather the Boston Area

Faculty Group on Public Issues (BAFGOPI), centred at MIT, as most regional peace activism was (see pp. 114–5), at the outset devoted to disarmament issues. I did not become 'an adviser', and in fact had joined it years earlier, as soon as it was founded by my close friend and fellow activist biologist (Nobel laureate) Salvador Luria. And it was indeed small, as one would expect of a regional faculty peace group, and as is surely true of others (if there were any like it at the time; not to my knowledge). Its activism extended to many protests it organised nationwide. But the major anti-war activism on campus was not BAFGOPI, but what I described earlier (pp. 5–6).

Let us put these fantasies aside and turn to the den of iniquity itself: the Research Lab of Electronics (RLE) in the famous Building 20, well known as a rich and lively interdisciplinary centre from which several departments developed – linguistics, philosophy, psychology and others – as MIT was making the transition from an engineering school to a science-based university with distinguished departments in the humanities and social sciences. RLE housed a small project on machine translation (MT), to which I was appointed in 1955, along with several other linguists. Following his consistent practice, Knight once again scrupulously ignores what is plainly the most relevant evidence relating to his charges: what were they actually doing? So I will fill in the gaps.

The project was headed by physicist Victor Yngve, who was genuinely interested in MT, as was a regular visitor, Israeli philosopher-logician Yehoshua Bar-Hillel, who published widely on the topic. Neither had a thought of any military application, nor did anyone else on the project, and in retrospect, it is uncontroversial that there never was any.

Knight concedes that I had no interest in MT; rather, I continued the work I had been doing since my undergraduate years. The other linguists on the project were GH Matthews (working on the first large-scale generative grammar, of the Amerindian language Hidatsa), RB Lees (studying Turkish nominalisations, his PhD dissertation, the first in our programme) and F Lukoff (grammar of Korean). All of us were also continuing our work on linguistic theory and the structure of English. Several of us also worked closely with the other linguist at RLE, Morris Halle, who was pursuing his investigations of acoustic phonetics and Russian phonology, often in collaboration with Roman Jakobson, who came to MIT after retiring from Harvard in 1967. In the early 60s, we were joined by John Viertel, who was engaged in translation and analysis of classic work of Wilhelm von Humboldt, and shortly after by the remarkable linguist and cultural anthropologist Kenneth Hale, under whose leadership our programme became a leading international centre for the study of Australian, Native American and other indigenous languages, along with work on indigenous land rights, establishing cultural centres, bringing students from indigenous communities to study at MIT, etc. Other faculty also joined, working on a wide range of similar topics, as can easily be determined by the publications that Knight avoids.

Military significance? Zero. Social and political consequences? Actually quite a lot. Small wonder that Knight ignores it all, just as he completely evades the fact, discussed earlier, that RLE, along with MIT generally, was the regional centre of Vietnam War protest and, from 1965, direct resistance (academics among the founders and board members of the national organisation RESIST, for example, were primarily from MIT, particularly RLE).

The pattern continues, sometimes with deceit so petty that one can only gasp in disbelief. Take for example his discussion of the important issue of the two military labs that were formally administered by MIT, though separate from the academic programme. As discussed at the conference (pp. 115–6), as activism developed in the late 60s, two positions emerged on how to deal with the labs: roughly, the 'left-wing position' (me and a few others) that the formal relation should be maintained, for the reasons discussed at the conference; and the 'right-wing position' that they should be formally separated – Knight's position.[34]

In his heroic effort to confuse the issue, Knight reports (page 67, note 7) that 'Chomsky was well aware of what was going on at his university. As he said, "I'm at MIT, so I'm always talking to the scientists who work on missiles for the Pentagon." Or again: "There was extensive weapons research on the MIT campus.... In fact, a good deal of the [nuclear] missile guidance technology was developed right on the MIT campus and in laboratories run by the university"'.

Damning no doubt, until we check his source and once again find carefully contrived deceit. The taped conversation that he unearthed with considerable effort is not about MIT itself, but about the military lab near the campus, the I-Lab (now Draper Laboratory). It was 'run by the university' in the manner I discussed: under joint administration, while entirely separate from the academic programme, where there was no classified work at all. The phrase 'MIT campus' is used here informally, as was standard, to include the military labs that were separate from the actual campus.

A major theme of Knight's tale, here and in earlier publications, is that I was facing incredible pressures from the directors and inhabitants of the den of iniquity at the 'heart of the empire', and he praises me effusively for my courage in somehow managing to resist it while contriving my exotic brand of linguistics to assuage my conscience for working for the American military machine.

He provides not a particle of evidence about the pressures, and, as usual, provides us with the refutation of his claims, this time in the actual text, not just in footnotes that we have to investigate to reveal the conscious deceit. By 1967, he writes, 'MIT's managers had given Chomsky a named professorship which, as he recalls, "isolated me from the alumni and government pressures"'. This was *after* I had – very publicly – moved from my active involvement in anti-war protest in earlier years to direct resistance – for which I was in fact facing a federal trial. Though of course one could not publicly go into detail on these matters, I did give some indication of the range of resistance activities in which I and others were involved in a 1967 essay ('On Resistance'), reprinted in a collection that includes 'RoI' and others from the same time or before, and dedicated to 'the brave young men who refuse to serve in a criminal war'.[35]

I could go on to detail how supportive 'MIT's managers' were not only of me personally, but of the department generally, including all of us who were intensively engaged in political action, including very public resistance activities. Same throughout the Institute. Another pillar of Knight's construction crumbles, this time on minimal inspection.[36]

There should be no need to proceed to dismantle further the web of deceit and misinformation that Knight spins, though at least a few words are necessary about the two individuals he specifically maligns, the two figures whose photos he selected to post. One is John Deutch, who 'brought biological warfare research to the university in the 1980s', and may have even gone 'so far as to pressure junior faculty into performing this research "on campus"'[37]. Very serious charges, certainly. Checking Knight's footnote, we find that his sole source is an unsourced statement in an underground newspaper that he mis-describes as 'the student newspaper.' More impressive scholarship.

His second example, Jerome Wiesner, is far more important. Wiesner was director of RLE, then became John F. Kennedy's science adviser, then returned to MIT as provost and later president. So he was my 'boss' for several decades, Knight declares. Knight seems to know as little about research institutions and universities as, it seems, about political activism. The director of a lab, or the provost and president of a university, is not the 'boss' of anyone. That's not how the institutions work. There should be no need to elaborate.

Once again, Knight's footnotes provide ample material to flatly refute the defamatory tale he spins of a leading warmonger.

Opening Knight's primary source on Wiesner,[38] we discover a highly knowledgeable account of his actual activities both at MIT and in the government – an account from the left, by physicist Philip Morrison, a McCarthy target who was forced to curtail his non-academic activities[39] and then came to MIT, where he was free to pursue them. Morrison describes Wiesner as

> one of MIT's most effective reforming presidents. The years of his presidency yielded lasting student diversity (women now comprise more than 40 percent of undergraduates [there were virtually none before]) and a widened range of opportunities for creative teaching and research, reaching the arts, spanning the humanities, and including the serious study of science and technology in their relation to society.[40]

Morrison also reviews Wiesner's leading role, while in the government, in bringing about the Partial Test Ban Treaty, which 'stopped the rapid and disastrous trend while levels [of fallout] were still tolerable', though it did not 'end the arms race – as Jerry, I, and others had hoped'.[41] The same source, which Knight was again kind enough to cite, provides ample evidence of Wiesner's initiatives on disarmament and arms control from the 50s and, as Kennedy's science adviser, and on to later years, all work for which he is quite well known.

And all ignored by Knight, who instead concocts a fairy tale about Wiesner's role in creating the missile gap. In fact, Wiesner's role was so slight that he is not even mentioned in authoritative insider accounts of the missile gap.[42] He was one of the scientists who investigated Air Force intelligence that did indeed indicate that there was a missile gap. But – crucially – he was the first to bring to the attention of Defence Secretary Robert McNamara that the intelligence was flawed, leading McNamara to recognise that 'There is no missile gap'.[43]

To support his charges, Knight cites Wiesner's report to incoming President Kennedy on 10 January 1961, in which he reviewed the consensus of all of the scientists that there was a missile gap, also calling for peaceful exploration of space. But the actual facts, mentioned above, he totally conceals. Again, Knight's prize charge collapses as soon as we look at his own sources.

Knight posts a photo he found of Wiesner in 1961, when he was Kennedy's science adviser, standing next to Defence Secretary McNamara, the implication being 'you know what *that* means'. And, revealingly, he omits Wiesner's crucial communication to McNamara explaining that there was no missile gap, his one significant contribution on this matter.

What is striking is the unfailing regularity with which Knight's vulgar exercises of defamation crash to the ground on a moment's inquiry, typically into the sources he provides. I can only assume that Knight provided these extensive sources in a show of scholarship, assuming that few would actually look into them. What precedes illustrates the pattern very clearly.

So it continues, paragraph after paragraph. It is unpleasant to permit the defamation and deceit to stand without comment. But perhaps this is enough to reveal the character of what Knight is doing. If any reader is interested in what I've put to the side here, I'll be glad to discuss it. And meanwhile I apologise for wasting time and space on this performance.

A detailed reply entitled 'My Response to Chomsky's Extraordinary Accusations' is available on Chris Knight's website, www.scienceandrevolution.org

Notes

1   Michel Crozier, Samuel Huntington and Joji Watanuki, *The Crisis of Democracy: Report on the Governability of Democracies to the Trilateral Commission* (New York: New York University Press, 1975).
2   Henry Kissinger, *American Foreign Policy: Three Essays* (New York: Norton, 1969), 28.
3   For discussion, see Noam Chomsky, *Deterring Democracy* (London: Verso, 1991), ch. 12.
4   Lewis F. Powell, Jr, 'Confidential memorandum: Attack of American free enterprise system,' 23 August 1971, available online at http://reclaimdemocracy.org/powell_memo_lewis/ (accessed 19 October 2018).
5   John Coatsworth, 'The Cold War in Central America, 1975–1991,' in Melvyn P. Leffler and Odd Arne Westad, eds, *Cambridge History of the Cold War* (Cambridge: Cambridge University Press, 2010).
6   Antonio Rubio, 'El Estado Mayor de El Salvador ordenó "eliminar" a Ignacio Ellacuría,' *El Mundo* (Spain), 22 November 2009. http://www.elmundo.es/elmundo/2009/11/21/espana/1258830475.html. This crucial document has yet to be mentioned in the US, to my knowledge, apart from publications from the wild men in the wings.
7   Quoted by Jon Reed, New York *Guardian* (now defunct), 23 May 1990. The quotation also appears in Noam Chomsky, *On Nature and Language* (Cambridge: Cambridge University Press, 2002), 166.
8   Tony Platt, *Beyond These Walls: Rethinking Crime and Punishment in the United States* (New York: St Martin's Press, 2019).
9   Anthony Lewis, 'Look on my works…,' *New York Times*, 1 May 1975, https://www.nytimes.com/1975/05/01/archives/look-on-my-works.html; Anthony Lewis, 'Ghosts,' *New York Times*, 27 December 1979, https://www.nytimes.com/1979/12/27/archives/abroad-at-home-ghosts.html
10 For a comprehensive scholarly review, see Clinton Fernandes, *The Independence of East Timor* (Brighton: Sussex Academic Press, 2011). In the US, the worst offender, even the basic facts are still denied in prestigious circles, a topic that merits much fuller analysis.

11 See for example Samantha Power's *A Problem from Hell: America and the Age of Genocide* (New York: Basic Books, 2002), a highly regarded multiple-award-winning study of our failure to deal with the other fellow's crimes (our own are scrupulously avoided). On East Timor, she criticises Washington for having 'looked away'. In fact, it looked right there, intensely, and expedited the slaughter effectively from the start.

12 See, among others, Thomas Ferguson, *Golden Rule: The Investment Theory of Party Competition and the Logic of Money-Driven Political Systems* (Chicago: University of Chicago Press, 1995); Martin Gilens, *Affluence and Influence: Economic Inequality and Political Power in America* (Princeton, NJ: Princeton University Press, 2012).

13 For many examples, see Chomsky, *Failed States*, ch. 5 (New York: Metropolitan Books, 2006); Sam Fleming, 'Battle lines: the fight for a fair vote in America,' *The Financial Times*, 2 August 2018.

14 'Berned out,' *The Economist*, 7 June 2018, https://www.economist.com/united-states/2018/06/07/berned-out; Ashley Kirzinger, Bryan Wu and Mollyann Brodie, 'Kaiser Health tracking poll – March 2018: Views on prescription drug pricing and Medicare-for-all proposals,' KFF: Henry J Kaiser Family Foundation, 23 March 2018, https://www.kff.org/health-reform/poll-finding/kaiser-health-tracking-poll-march-2018-prescription-drug-pricing-medicare-for-all-proposals/. *Morning Consult* and Politico, 'National tracking poll #170911: Crosstabulation results.' *Morning Consult*, 14–17 September 2017, https://morningconsult.com/wp-content/uploads/2017/09/170911_crosstabs_Politico_LIM_v1_AP-1.pdf

15 Daniel Chomsky, 'A distorting mirror: Major media coverage of Americans' tax policy preferences,' Institute for New Economic Thinking, April 2018, https://www.ineteconomics.org/research/research-papers/a-distorting-mirror-major-media-coverage-of-americans-tax-policy-preferences

16 Nelson D. Schwartz and Ben Casselman, 'Workers hardest hit by recession are joining in recovery,' *New York Times*, 3 August 2018, https://www.nytimes.com/2018/08/03/business/economy/july-jobs-report-2018.html

17 Familiar, and occasionally studied in some depth in the professional literature: Luigi Zingales, 'Towards a political theory of the firm,' *Journal of Economic Perspectives* 31, no. 3 (2017).

18 'Margaret Thatcher in quotes.' *The Spectator*, 8 April 2013, https://blogs.spectator.co.uk/2013/04/margaret-thatcher-in-quotes/

19 One correction. Rai cites the book *Manufacturing Consent* as Chomsky–Herman. At my insistence, we departed from our usual convention of alphabetical order in joint work and listed it as 'Herman and Chomsky', since the main framework was developed by the late Edward Herman, an old friend and frequent co-author.

20 Daniel Ellsberg, *The Doomsday Machine: Confessions of a Nuclear War Planner* (New York: Bloomsbury, 2017). His list goes to 1996, and he adds that there have been more since.

21 STRATCOM, *Essentials of Post-Cold War Deterrence*, 1995. http://www.nukestrat.com/us/stratcom/SAGessentials.PDF. For extensive quotes, see Noam Chomsky, *The New Military Humanism: Lessons From Kosovo* (Monroe, ME: Common Courage, 1999).

22 Harold Brown, Department of Defense Annual Report Fiscal Year 1981, https://history.defense.gov/Portals/70/Documents/annual_reports/1981_DoD_AR.pdf?ver=2014-06-24-150845-130 (accessed 14 November 2018).

23 General Lee Butler, 'Death by deterrence,' *Resurgence* 193 (March/April 1999), https://dwij.org/forum/statesperson/general_lee_butler.htm

24 Mary Ellen O'Connell, 'Unlawful killing with combat drones: A case study of Pakistan, 2004–2009,' *Notre Dame Law School, Legal Studies Research Paper* 09-43, July 2010. https://papers.ssrn.com/sol3/papers.cfm?abstract_id=1501144. See also, among others, the harsh indictment of Obama's use of combat drones in International Human Rights and Conflict Resolution Clinic at Stanford Law School and Global Justice Clinic at NYU School of Law, 'Living under drones: Death, injury and trauma to civilians from US drone practices in Pakistan,' 2012, https://www-cdn.law.stanford.edu/wp-content/uploads/2015/07/Stanford-NYU-Living-Under-Drones.pdf

25 Bernard Porter, reviewing Richard Gott's study of British crimes until 1858 – with plenty of horrors still to come. 'Schooled in anarchy,' *Times Literary Supplement*, 6 January 2012, https://www.the-tls.co.uk/articles/private/schooled-in-anarchy/

26 James Reston, 'Washington: Thanksgiving Day, 1967,' *New York Times*, 24 November 1967.

27 Noam Chomsky, 'Chomsky says,' *London Review of Books* 39, no. 12 (2017), https://www.lrb. co.uk/v39/n12/letters#letter4; Noam Chomsky, 'Chomsky has the last say,' *London Review of Books* 39, no. 16 (2017), https://www.lrb.co.uk/v39/n16/letters

28 Noam Chomsky, 'Chomsky says,' *London Review of Books* 39, no. 12 (2017), https://www.lrb. co.uk/v39/n12/letters#letter4; Noam Chomsky, 'Chomsky has the last say,' *London Review of Books* 39, no. 16 (2017), https://www.lrb.co.uk/v39/n16/letters

29 Noam Chomsky, *Morphophonemics of Modern Hebrew*, revised edition (New York: Garland, 1979 [1949, 1951]; Noam Chomsky, *The Logical Structure of Linguistic Theory*, revised edition (New York: Plenum, 1975 [1955, 1956]). See also several published articles on generative grammar.

30 Noam Chomsky, *Current Issues in Linguistic Theory* (The Hague: Mouton, 1964); Noam Chomsky, *Aspects of the Theory of Syntax* (Cambridge, MA: MIT Press, 1965); Noam Chomsky, *Cartesian Linguistics: A Chapter in the History of Rationalist Thought* (New York: Harper & Row, 1966); Noam Chomsky, *Language and Mind* (New York: Harcourt, Brace and World, 1968).

31 Nathaniel Rich and George Steinmetz, 'Losing earth: The decade we almost stopped climate change,' *New York Times*, 1 August 2018, https://www.nytimes.com/interactive/2018/08/01/magazine/climate-change-losing-earth.html

32 Editors' note: Chomsky is here responding to the draft of Knight's chapter he was asked to comment on, in which Keyser's rank was incorrectly described.

33 Wikipedia, 'Mike Mansfield,' https://en.wikipedia.org/wiki/Mike_Mansfield#Mansfield_Amendments

34 That is easily demonstrated. Once separated from MIT, the labs had the same status as Raytheon, ITEK and others doing military work, to which Knight expresses no objection.

35 Chomsky, *American Power and the New Mandarins* (1969).

36 Evidently recognising the self-refutation, Knight adds: 'But, despite this, his retraction suggests that he was still facing pressure from somewhere, presumably from his own colleagues at MIT'. The 'retraction' is another of Knight's gross distortions of a statement that is nothing of the sort. As any political activist is aware, dissidence invariably elicits opposition, and in my case it's easy enough to document it from the printed record. And there has been plenty more, but nothing of any moment at MIT, for me or other activists, again contrary to Knight's unsupported fabrications.

37 Editors' note: Chomsky is here responding to the draft of Knight's chapter he was asked to comment on, which included a reference to claims by student activists that John Deutch pressured junior faculty into performing mycotoxin research.

38 Rosenblith (ed.), *Jerry Wiesner* (2003).

39 Wikipedia, 'Philip Morrison,' https://en.wikipedia.org/wiki/Philip_Morrison#Activism

40 Rosenblith (ed.), *Jerry Wiesner* (2003), 59.

41 Rosenblith (ed.), *Jerry Wiesner* (2003).

42 Ellsberg, *Doomsday Machine* (2017).

43 Rosenblith (ed.), *Jerry Wiesner* (2003), 285. Or rather, as the new evidence that Wiesner provided to McNamara revealed, there was a substantial 'missile gap' – in Washington's favour. See Ellsberg, *Doomsday Machine* (2017).

8

Conference Q&A

Noam Chomsky

This question-and-answer session is from the conference held at UCL on 25 February 2017, commemorating the 50th anniversary of the publication of 'The Responsibility of Intellectuals'.

CHAIR (CHRIS KNIGHT): Could you comment on the responsibility of intellectuals in the light of Donald Trump and the contemporary political scene?

NOAM CHOMSKY: Well the problems are the same, and pretty much have been ever since the term 'intellectual' came to be used in its contemporary sense. About the time of the Dreyfus trial, there was a small group of Dreyfusards who defended Dreyfus. Émile Zola was the most famous. As usual, they were bitterly condemned by the intellectual elites, by the great figures of the Académie Française and by others. How dare these writers and journalists condemn the great institutions of our society – the state, the army! Émile Zola had to in fact flee France to avoid prosecution. That's the pretty general story.

A couple of years later came the First World War. When the war broke out, on all sides intellectuals enthusiastically supported the war effort of their own country. The famous declaration of, I think, about 90 leading German intellectuals explaining to the intellectual community of the world the nobility of the course that Germany was following, citing great figures – Kant, Beethoven, and so on. Same in every other country. In England and the United States, the intellectuals enthusiastically rallied to the cause.

In the United States, the most enthusiastic supporters were the liberal intellectuals of the John Dewey circles. To his credit, I should say,

Dewey years later did change his position but at that time, again enthusiastic support for the war. Woodrow Wilson had won the election in 1916 on the slogan of 'Peace without victory,' but immediately dedicated himself to victory without peace, and it was necessary to carry out a huge propaganda campaign to drive a basically pacifist population to war fever. And the intellectuals were in the lead championing the cause of war. Dewey and others wrote at the time that this is the first time in history in the United States that a war had been called not by militarists and business circles but by the leading thinkers in the country who had made a deliberate, careful decision that this was the most rational direction to pursue and so on.

There were dissidents. So Bertrand Russell in England, Karl Liebknecht and Rosa Luxemburg in Germany, Eugene Debs in the United States. They were in jail. Randolph Bourne, another anti-war intellectual, wasn't actually jailed in the United States but he was excluded from the liberal journals. That's the general pattern. It goes on right up through much of history. We can go back further, go back to classical Greece. The person who drank the hemlock was the one who was corrupting the youth of Athens by asking too many questions. And that's pretty much the standard throughout history and that remains the case now, but to a lesser extent actually.

It's important to recognise that the activism of the 1960s did have a civilising effect on society in many respects. A lot of institutional regression, but cultural progress. And by now the status and ability of dissidents to reach a broader audience has indeed improved from what it was in the early 1960s, the mid 1960s and back through history, though it still remains pretty marginal now. Donald Trump himself is kind of carrying out a very carefully calculated war against what are called the liberal media. As you probably heard, he excluded the *New York Times* and *CNN* from the latest press conference. The *Washington Post* – the other national newspaper – in protest refused to even send a reporter.

This is all throwing red meat to his constituency, trying to keep them fired up with the idea that they're somehow under attack by liberal elites, while he himself and his administration are slavishly following the demands of extreme wealth and power and organising programmes that will be extremely harmful to their own constituency and indeed to much of the country and the world. So in that context, the role of intellectuals, of people who are in a position to articulate publicly a position and point of view, of course that changes. But fundamentally, I think this picture runs pretty much through history – deviations here and there, changes in many ways, relaxation in more recent years, largely the result of the civilising effect of the 1960s which was considerable.

CHAIR: You have recently said that Donald Trump's tearing up of the climate science agreements may be 'the death knell of the human species'. In that context, what do you think is the responsibility of the climate scientists around the world who know very well what horrendous dangers are involved in reaching a tipping point with global warming, perhaps at some point even the possibility of the Amazon rainforest catching fire and the whole planet becoming pretty much uninhabitable. What is the responsibility of scientists? Should they get self-organised and resist?

NOAM CHOMSKY: There had been of course Pugwash, which was concerned with nuclear weapons. That goes back to the early days of the nuclear age. But in general scientists had been pretty passive and quiet. Starting in the late 1960s, mainly, in fact at first at MIT and then elsewhere, organisations of scientists did form which became more active in the general public domain, trying to reach the public with important issues of scientific significance.

The main one, the Union of Concerned Scientists, was the direct outgrowth of the protests at MIT, student and faculty protests in 1968/69. And climate scientists understood by the early 1970s that we were facing a pretty serious problem. In fact I can remember very well, back in the early 1970s, being told privately by two personal friends – one of them the head of earth sciences at Harvard, the other the head of meteorology at MIT – that recent information that they'd got was pretty dire. That was the early 1970s. By the 1980s there were the beginnings of more organised protest, by now quite a lot. And climate scientists, and in fact scientists generally, certainly have a responsibility to make the public aware as much as they can of the significance of scientific results. But it's not just *their* responsibility. It's everybody's responsibility. We are now facing a real existential crisis. The possibility that organised human life may continue on anything like the scale that we now know is very much threatened.

Maybe people think that there's a refugee problem now. That's nothing like what it'll be when, say, the sea level rises enough so that the coastal plains of Bangladesh will be flooded and tens of millions, if not hundreds of millions of people will be fleeing. The glaciers in the Himalayas may melt and threaten the water supply of South Asia. It could be a horrendous outcome – even possibly a nuclear war arising between two nuclear-armed states who'll be struggling to control their diminishing water supplies.

The effects of climate change have already been playing quite a significant role in exacerbating some of the major conflicts in the world. The atrocities in Darfur were to a substantial extent a result of the extreme drought which was driving nomadic groups into agricultural areas leading to major conflicts and the terribly atrocities there. Or take the Syrian war, one of the worst modern catastrophes. Part of the background was an unprecedented drought, not known for thousands of years of history, which simply decimated Syrian agriculture growth, drove peasants into urban slums, set the basis for tension and conflict, which erupted when the flame was lit, and this is going to happen more and more. Meanwhile, coastal cities are threatened, the effects of the environmental changes are going to be drastic, and not in the far distance.

So what's the responsibility of everyone? Well, to try to avert this catastrophe. We know of ways to mitigate it, maybe reverse it, and some steps are being taken, nowhere near enough, but at least some. However, there is an extremely serious danger. Let's go back to 8 November, when several important events took place.

One was not only the election of Donald Trump but the takeover of all three branches of government by the Republican Party, which I have called – and I will repeat – the most dangerous organisation in human history, and I think that's regarded as an outrageous statement but it is in fact quite accurate. They are dedicated to racing as quickly as possible towards the precipice. And there was a second event on 8 November, more important than the election I think.

There was an international UN-sponsored conference, COP22, in Marrakesh, Morocco. Its mission was to try to put some teeth into the Paris negotiations of a year earlier, COP21. The Paris negotiations had not been able to a reach a verifiable treaty, for a simple reason: the Republican Congress would not approve it, so it therefore was left with voluntary agreements. COP22 in Morocco was going to try to spell out the results. The conference proceeded until 8 November. On 8 November the conference pretty much stopped, and the rest of it was devoted to trying to face the fact that the most powerful, wealthy country in world history was now withdrawing, formally, from the effort to try to deal with climate change.

That's a huge problem for everyone – not just for Americans, but for everyone else. So the task that is faced is not simply for climate scientists – their job is to present to the public the information that's available – but for everyone else to try to stop this race to disaster, which is not very far off in the distance.

QUESTIONER 1: Your idea of the doctrine of good intentions states that anything that the West engages in, in a military sense, is done from a position of a moral, noble stance, inherently. What would you recommend are the best methods of countering this kind of foundational propaganda that provides, in effect, moral cover for extreme and horrendous crimes?

NOAM CHOMSKY: To qualify slightly, it's not just the West. It's every powerful force in history. So take, say, Japan during its conquests in mainland Asia and east Asia in the 1930s and the 1940s. The Japanese were carrying out horrendous atrocities. The rape of Nanking, all sorts of massacres, torture and destruction. But we have internal documents from Japan, released by US intelligence back in the 1960s, which are their internal discussions of what they're doing, not propaganda. And the rhetoric is so uplifting it brings tears to your eyes. They're engaged in trying to bring about an 'earthly paradise' – that's the phrase that was used – to protect the people of China from the Chinese bandits who were trying to prevent Japan from bringing its magnificent technological achievements and advances to the backward people of Asia, and so on. That's fascist Japan.

When Hitler took over the Sudetenland, same story. He was going to end ethnic conflicts, bring to the people the benefits of superior German civilisation, and so on. In fact, I think it'd be hard to find a case in history when some powerful, dominant group did not construct an ideological framework to justify what it was doing as pure benevolence in the interests of the people who were being saved. And this is true, even of the most respected, advanced thinkers.

Take, say, John Stuart Mill. Hard to find a person in modern history who was more thoughtful, intelligent, progressive and so on. But read his article on intervention, famous article on intervention, which is actually taught in law schools and others. It's considered an anti-interventionist article. But when you read it, it's a little different. What he said is England is an unusual, a unique power. It's kind of an angelic power, there's been nothing like it in history. In fact England is so angelic that others don't understand us. When we carry out our actions abroad, we are subjected to obloquy and continental commentators accuse us of base motives because they can't appreciate how magnificent we are.

He was focusing on India at the time. The question was should England intervene in India? And he gave measured arguments one way or another and finally concluded that even though we will be denounced for having base intentions by people who can't understand our nobility, nevertheless we must intervene in India and continue the conquest of India. That was essentially the message.

Take a look at the time. It was 1859, right after the Indian uprising, called in England the 'Indian mutiny', which was suppressed with extreme violence and brutality by the British forces. It was not a secret matter, it was discussed openly in Parliament, and liberals like Richard Cobden bitterly condemned it, but mainly it was supported. And John Stuart Mill was a functionary of the East India Company, he knew exactly what was going on. The reason for the continued conquest of India was not to protect the barbarians and provide them with a superior civilisation, it was an effort to try and gain control of – if possible – a monopoly of the opium trade so that Britain could force its way into China. The Second Opium War was taking place by means of guns and drugs, the only method England had to break into China and compel them to take British manufactures.

Well, that was the context, and that's one of the most impressive intellectual figures you can think of in the modern period. So it's very broad, this phenomenon. How do you deal with it? By trying to expose it. By bringing out the actual facts. And to an extent that's been done.

Go back to the 1960s again and take the case you mentioned, the conquest of the Americas. It was the general view in the 1960s – among scholars, incidentally, great anthropologists and others – that in the western hemisphere there were maybe a million people, hunter-gatherers, straggling around a backward area and, first the Spanish, and then the English invaders – not invaders, liberators – were bringing civilisation, order and progress to this fundamentally empty territory. It's true that some of the people there suffered from it, but it was partly a result of their own savagery.

If you read the US Declaration of Independence, for example, written by Thomas Jefferson – again, one of the leading Enlightenment figures – one of the accusations, there was a litany of accusations against King George III, and one of them, recited piously every year on 4 July, is that the King of England unleashed against us the merciless Indian savages whose known way of warfare is torture and violence – and of course we had to defend ourselves. Jefferson was right there on the scene. He knew perfectly well, at least in a corner of his mind, that it was the merciless *English* savages whose known way of warfare was violence and brutality and were conquering and destroying the country.

That was pretty much the picture in the 1960s. If you took a course at a university that's what you learned. In more recent years that's been changed. Scholarship now recognises, and much of the public now understands, that the picture is radically false. There weren't a million hunter-gatherers straggling around. There were maybe 80 million people with advanced civilisations, in many respects more advanced than Europe, complex agricultural developments, big cities, lots of trade between south and north, careful nurturing and control of what was called a wilderness and was anything but. And what actually happened was the worst genocide in human history, very quickly.

So consciousness has to a large extent been changed by a lot of activist work. It didn't happen just by some miracle. There were some scholars, many activists, native Americans and many others who finally brought about a substantial – not complete – change in understanding.

And to go back to your question, that's the way it has to be done on every single issue. And it's pretty striking that in quite recent years there has been a real awakening on the two major crimes of the European colonisation and British colonisation of the Americas: the virtual extermination of the indigenous populations and the most vicious system of slavery that was ever created – which is in fact the source of a lot of the wealth of Britain, the United States and, indirectly, the continent. Of course cotton was the fuel of the early industrial revolution and the hideous plantation system of the South, which was economically pretty efficient, was supplying this source of manufacturing, finance, commerce, retail, particularly in England and the United States but elsewhere as well.

This is beginning, finally, to be understood, and a lot of it is the work of intellectuals and much is the work of activists and organisers. People try to bring this kind of understanding to the general public, including the victims: Native Americans, black activists and others have always been quite prominent in trying to break through these ugly and disgraceful misinterpretations, and the same is true on other issues. So we know how to proceed, the question is organising the energy to be able to carry it out.

QUESTIONER 2 (JACKIE WALKER): You very kindly sent me a message of support because of the campaign of vilification that I've had in terms of being a supporter of Palestinian rights, and I thank you very much for doing that. I want to ask you about what I see as a real threat to our democracy, certainly in the UK, through a couple of things. One is the monoculture and the laziness of our media, which tends to only tell one story, and one very controlled story, and the second is the apparently increasingly corrupt political system we have, where we only seem to have the choice given to us by the people who actually do the choosing of how we should live and what we should say.

NOAM CHOMSKY: Well, again, nothing new about this. I mentioned the reaction of the liberal *Boston Globe* to the first anti-war demonstrations in the Boston area, and this is a pattern that goes through a long period of history. There are changes and modifications. The same is true of the political system. There's a constant struggle to try to open up the institutions of the society, whether media or government, to more direct responsiveness to the needs and goals of the general population. Sometimes there are successes, sometimes there are failures, there's regression and progress.

In the case of the political system, actually Britain is somewhat more progressive than the United States is. In Britain, it is possible to be a member of the Labour Party and to play some kind of role in the shaping of the positions and so on. In the United States there are no political parties of that kind. You can't be a member of the Democratic Party, you can't be a participant in setting up its positions and so on. The parties have evolved since the nineteenth century as basically candidate-producing organisations in which you can push a lever once every four years. But the effort to create real, popular-based parties in which people create, construct the programmes and decisions – beginning on the local level all the way up – that's a major task. And there is some progress in that respect.

So, one pretty striking development in the United States, just in the last election, was the remarkable achievements of the Bernie Sanders campaign. In the United States – not all that different from elsewhere but a more extreme case – elections are basically bought. Political scientists have shown you can predict the outcome of an election with remarkable precision simply by looking at campaign spending – and by the same factor, campaign spending is highly determinative of the policies that are pursued. Sanders broke this pattern for the first time in well over a century.

Here's somebody, an unknown figure (a senator, but few people knew him), calling himself a socialist (which used to be a scare word in the United States; still is to a large extent), basically calling for New Deal policies, a big change from the neoliberal repression since Reagan and Thatcher: no corporate funding, no business funding, no funding from the wealthy, no media support. He would have won the Democratic nomination if it hadn't been for shenanigans internal to the party system. Among younger people, so-called millennials, he was overwhelmingly favoured.

This is a remarkable achievement, and it gives an indication of what can be done to develop authentic politics. As far as the media are concerned, it's a complex story but in many ways I think the media are somewhat more open to critical and independent discussion than they were 40 or 50 years ago. On the other hand, there's been a monopolisation and a narrowing of media sources, which goes in the other direction. But there are other forms of media available now, through the internet which gives an opportunity for many independent voices. And I think there are plenty of opportunities to pursue, to deal with the very real and significant questions and issues that you bring up.

QUESTIONER 3: Around the early 1990s we saw a sudden relaxation of the atmosphere after the Thatcher–Reagan stranglehold on any kind of thinking, when the intelligentsia moved – with a few notable exceptions of course – to the right and all the wonderful free radical spirits of the 1960s and 1970s suddenly became born-again free marketeers. And I think that when Clinton arrived it captured the mood, although it took five years in the UK for the Labour Party to arrive, there was certainly a relaxation of the atmosphere, even if they still went around thumping Third World countries.

Now I see that there is a resurgence of that kind of feeling and it is worrying me very greatly in the sense that it's perfectly alright to make prejudiced comments, to say something which is racist, anti-immigrant. And you can tell that this is not something that is true but it is sort of simply like a factoid is being created. And if we look to countries like India – a few countries where you thought that there was something like an independent democratic process – the legislators are trying to out-Trump Trump and saying if there are refugees then we won't take them if they're of a certain religion unless they meet certain criteria. So, wherever we look in the world, there is the right-wing being on the ascendancy in a very aggressive way. Where's it all going to end, and why is it so hard to make liberal and progressive values stick?

NOAM CHOMSKY: Well first of all, I have a considerably less rosy view of the 1990s, both in England and the United States. Putting that aside, you're quite right that there is an outburst in much of the world now of extreme, very dangerous, far-right, racist, xenophobic and other tendencies. In many ways, I think it's more threatening and dangerous in Europe, especially continental Europe, than it is in the United States. It's bad enough in the United States, but take continental Europe:

In the last Austrian election, a figure who comes out of a neo-Nazi background came very close to winning the presidential election, missed by a hair. That's Austria, where we have some memories about Nazism. In Germany, the Alternative for Germany, the right-wing alternative to the conservative Merkel government is gaining significant power, and we have some memories about Germany too. I'm old enough to remember listening to Hitler's speeches over the radio in the 1930s, not understanding the words as a child, but couldn't miss the thrust and the massive popular support, and so on. That's threatening.

Take a look at France. The next election that's coming in France will end up with two candidates: one, again an outgrowth of a neo-Nazi party, a neo-fascist party who has the most popularity in the country, the second was banned by the courts for various corruption charges. But assuming he runs, it's xenophobic, ultra-conservative reactionary. Those are the two choices in France. India is pretty much the same, and yes there's that phenomenon all over the world.

I think a lot of it can be traced back to the extremely harmful effects on most of the population of the world of the neoliberal policies that were in fact instituted, carried forward by Reagan and Thatcher and by their followers – that includes Clinton and Blair through the 1990s. And for much of the population this has been really harmful.

So, for example, in the United States, real wages for working people, in 2007, right before the crash – the peak of the so-called economic miracle – were lower than they were in 1979, literally lower than at the point when the neoliberal experiment began. Real wages for male workers in the United States are about in the 1960s. The black population has suffered immensely. About ten years ago, average wealth for the black population, which is pretty meagre, was about one tenth of the white population, now it's about one twentieth. What wealth there was virtually wiped out by the 2008 recession.

Plenty of things like that happen all over. I think a lot of them can be traced to the effect of the neoliberal policies that were instituted beginning, a little bit in the late 1970s, taking off under Reagan, Thatcher and others around the world. The so-called Washington Consensus imposed on much of the Third World was devastating. Latin

America lost decades of growth and development. But there is a reaction to it, there's a strong reaction and it's not just on the right. There's a progressive reaction too. So Podemos in Spain, the Sanders phenomenon in the United States, others elsewhere. Varoufakis' DiEM25 movement in continental Europe. These things exist and I think they're quite significant and have some hope for the future. The same is happening in India. It's a battle, a constant struggle all through history, ebbs and flows, forward and backward. And overall, in time, I think, to borrow Martin Luther King's famous phrase, 'the moral arc of history does somewhat bend towards justice', but not by itself. Only when it's pushed in that direction by dedicated, committed effort. And I think that's true right now, as it always has been.

QUESTIONER 4: This question is about your concept from five decades ago – 'The Responsibility of Intellectuals' – by which you meant responsibility to the public good. And that seminal article has generated crucial debate over these five decades on how this should be done, and how it isn't done, how intellectuals in many cases are silenced by fear or even corrupted by rewards.

But responsibility has just the opposite meaning as well. Earlier today we heard a talk about how MIT academics initiated the proposal for whole new weapons systems, supposedly in the name of defence, and somehow persuaded the Pentagon to spend enormous amounts of money on this with them as the chief experts, even contrary to the advice of military leaders. And this seems to be an extreme case of an insight you brought, namely that intellectuals identify with state power, especially with an oppressive state power. And earlier in your talk today you gave examples throughout history of how intellectuals not only identified with the problems of the powerful, but creatively expanded on those problems, in order to provide ambitious, creative solutions with them as the chief experts. So there's an impulse to become close to power, which is about something more than simply material rewards.

So I want to ask a question from your long experience of being both close and distant to such people who have served power, especially through systems of mass murder, since you got to know some of these people over several decades, what is the source of intellectuals' vicarious identification with oppressive power? What drives this identification and how can we draw on those insights to undermine such impulses to serve an oppressive power?

NOAM CHOMSKY: Well, as you mentioned and as I kind of indicated, there's a long history of this, going back as far as we'd like to go. I mentioned classical Greece. I could mention the Biblical record at roughly the same time.

There were in the Biblical record a group of people who we call 'prophets'. It's actually a dubious translation of an obscure Hebrew word, it didn't have much to do with prophesying. What were they saying? These were people giving critical geopolitical analysis, warning that the actions of the King were going to lead to disaster. They were calling for mercy for widows and orphans. They were pretty much what we would nowadays call dissident intellectuals in many respects. How were they treated? They were imprisoned, driven into the desert. The prophet Elijah was brought to King Ahab, the most vicious of the kings. The King denounced him as a hater of Israel because he was criticising the acts of the evil King. There were others at the same time who, centuries later, were called false prophets. They were the flatterers of the court. They were the privileged group, the ones who had access to power and privilege, wealth and so on. Many centuries later, the values were reversed. You honour the prophets, you condemn the false prophets. But that's centuries later.

Well that pattern, both in the Biblical record and classical Greece, goes right through history. I gave modern examples, and it's not hard to think of the reasons. I mean, if you're a scientist or a professor at a university or a student or a lawyer or whatever, you have choices. You can serve the interests of power and wealth and gain the same amenities yourself, gain privilege, gain respectability, all sorts of doors are open to you. Or you can be a critical dissident. In which case, you're likely to suffer one or another form of oppression. What kind depends on the country. So in the United States and England, you're not sent to a torture chamber. You're not sent to the gulag. But other things happen that kind of marginalise you in many ways. Your articles don't get published, you get condemned in public, you're kind of pushed aside, maybe you don't get a good job and that kind of thing. So the pressures are pretty obvious.

Support for power and privilege brings rewards, naturally. If you're a lawyer, you can be a public interest lawyer, work 70 hours a week trying to protect people who are vulnerable and in need and live on a pittance. Or you can join a corporate law firm and become quite wealthy and privileged and so on and so forth. Those are the kinds of choices that faced people all through history. So it's not all that surprising to see that, by and large – quite overwhelmingly, in fact – people of some education, privilege, the kind we call 'intellectuals', tend, by no means a hundred per cent, to be supportive of power and privilege.

It's also intellectually much easier to accept the common sense of the day, the common beliefs and doctrines, and not question them, than it is to expose them to critical examination. Easier in many ways. So for example, to be quite simple, if I were to say 'Al-Qaeda is a terrorist organisation', I don't even need any evidence. Just say it, it's fine, go ahead. Suppose I say that the United States is the leading terrorist power in the world. Well, it sounds kind of surprising. I've got to have evidence, and furthermore I have to have evidence at the level of physics, not just history. It's not that hard to show. But the task is incomparably more difficult than just playing along with the flow of doctrine and standard beliefs.

So for many reasons it's not hard to see why you find the tendencies that you do find. As I said, during the First World War, to take another example, if you were cheering patriotically for your own country, that was fine. If you decided to criticise it, say the way Bertrand Russell did or Rosa Luxemburg or Eugene Debs, you ended up in jail. OK, not too surprising to see which way things go. How do you combat it? The same way you combat other injustices, violence and repression in the society. By constant, dedicated work.

CHAIR: One of the intellectuals that you attacked very strongly in your article 'The Responsibility of Intellectuals', of course, was the MIT economic historian Walt Rostow. In the discussion this afternoon, other names came up: Jerome Wiesner, John Deutch. The previous question was driving at whether you had any personal experience of some of these people very close to power, advisers of, at that point, Lyndon Johnson.

NOAM CHOMSKY: Actually, I have very little experience with those groups. They are there, but the people at MIT who I knew most, who I knew well and worked with, were the ones on the opposite side, the dissidents and the critics. So for example, when Walt Rostow went to Washington to serve the administration, there was a Boston area faculty peace group which was centred at MIT. That was the centre of the most of the faculty anti-war activity. And the people involved were quite distinguished scientists. People like a very close friend, Salvador Luria, Nobel laureate in biology, others like that. That's the kind of circles in which I was. And the same with the student body.

The student body was quite conservative until the late 1960s. But there was a small group of students who were organising among the student body, a very small group. Those were the young people I was quite close to. They finally succeeded in pretty much taking over the university. What I described, the change in 1966, 1967, 1968, was largely the result of groups like these. And it became quite substantial. I mentioned that the resistance organisations – not just the protests, but the resistance organisations, which were a serious matter – were facing federal trials and so on; insofar as there was an academic contribution it was mostly coming from MIT.

By 1968, a small group of MIT students organised a sanctuary for a marine deserter; a couple of faculty were involved too, me as well. This literally shut down the campus for about two weeks. The campus was almost totally focused on protecting this marine deserter. In the student centre there were 24-hour seminars, music, all the kinds of 1960s activities. And it had a big impact. It led to the first serious discussion of the responsibility of technologists and scientists about the consequences of what they were doing. And there were outgrowths, like say the Union of Concerned Scientists and others, which changed the culture of the university. So inside the university, as elsewhere, there's constant struggle going on, and MIT was a particularly striking place.

Actually, contrary to what was often believed, MIT itself did not have war work, war-related work, on the campus. On the campus itself, there was a commission in 1969, the Pounds Commission, which reviewed this quite closely. There was no classified work on campus. There was no directly war-oriented work. Of course, anything that's done has some possible military applications. So work in anthropology, for example, was picked up by the military for counter-insurgency and so on.

MIT did administer two military laboratories, the Lincoln Lab and what was then called the I-Lab, now the Draper Lab working on counter-insurgency, on the guidance systems for intercontinental missiles and so on. They were administered by MIT but they were not on campus and there was a major struggle about it.

By the time the campus got politicised by the late 1960s, there was significant debate and struggle about the military labs and there were basically two positions. For convenience, the right-wing position was to keep, to move the labs, to break the relation, the formal relation, between MIT and the labs. That's the position that actually won.

The left position, of which I was a part in a small group of students, was to keep the labs connected to campus. We wanted them to retain the formal relationship. And the reason was very simple. If they were moved off campus formally, everything would proceed exactly as before without visibility. If they were formally connected to the campus, to the academic programme, there would be a constant source of educational activity, protest, activism to try to end their activities. Well, that was basically the struggle; the right-wing position won. Now they're formally separated from the campus.

But MIT itself doesn't have war work. In fact the only exception was at that time the political science department, which did have direct involvement in counterinsurgency activity in Vietnam. But that's the kind of struggle that goes on at MIT. It was quite an interesting place in that respect.

QUESTIONER 5: I mean to ask you about Trump and Cuba. When Obama did a deal with Cuba, you mentioned the real reasons behind the deal. And if Trump pulls out of the deal and changes his policies, do you think they will isolate the United States from it and that we'll have some of the Latin American countries stop being the dog working for the US?

NOAM CHOMSKY: Well that's an interesting question and the answer is, for the moment, unknown. He hasn't said anything. To go into the background a little bit: the United States has of course been totally isolated in the world on the harsh embargo against Cuba. There were major terrorist attacks against Cuba, primarily during the Kennedy administration, and then continued, and these have been kind of marginalised in history. You have to really work to find out about them. They're a large part of the reason for the Cuban missile crisis, in fact. But, take a look at the votes at the United Nations on the US embargo. It's practically unanimous, by now actually unanimous against the United States, apart from Israel. But, more significantly, inside the hemisphere the United States was becoming isolated.

As the countries of mainly South America, but to some extent Central America, started to extricate themselves from the neoliberal disaster and from the traditional control of the imperial powers – in the last century, the United States – they began to take quite an independent course. There are no US military bases left in South America. The International Monetary Fund, which is basically an agency of the US Treasury Department, has been expelled from South America. It works in Europe, not in South America. And the new hemispheric organisations that were being founded were beginning to exclude the United States.

CELAC [The Community of Latin American and Caribbean States] includes the entire hemisphere apart from the United States and Canada. And there are regular hemispheric summit meetings. At the last one, in Cartagena, the United States and Canada were isolated totally from the rest of the hemisphere, primarily on the issue of admitting Cuba into the hemispheric system. The next meeting was coming up in 2015 in Panama and it was pretty clear that the United States might simply be expelled from the hemisphere if the US persisted in its attacks on Cuba. So Obama made the sensible move of beginning to normalise relations with, of course, the usual rhetoric of how we're doing this for the benefit of the Cuban people and so on and so forth. But the motivation and policies were not that obscure, kept quiet by the media and commentary, but anybody who wanted to think about it could see it.

Well, what is Trump going to do? We don't know. There's been no comment or discussion so far. And I think it's not so clear. He's a very unpredictable figure. The Republican Party is a very strange organisation, it's mostly a kind of wrecking ball. We don't know what they're going to do next. But for the moment, at least, they have not indicated any particular policy decisions with regard to Cuba.

QUESTIONER 6: What is your perspective on the Palestinians' BDS [Boycott, Divestment, Sanctions] movement, and in particular what is the responsibility of the intellectuals and academics in respect to that particular movement?

NOAM CHOMSKY: First off, it's really BD. There are no sanctions at the moment. It may come to that, but at the moment there are no sanctions in prospect. The boycott and divestment proposals and the effort to initiate such policies was developed at first by an Israeli group, Gush Shalom. Uri Avnery is the leading figure. In 1997, they organised a campaign to boycott any products, any activities having to do with the settlements in the occupied territories. It continued from then. By the early 2000s, there were a number of such efforts, I was involved in them and others think it's a very good tactic. The BDS movement itself was founded later, around 2005, and has its own programme and objectives. There are several distinct strands as to how to proceed with these efforts. One of them is like the Gush Shalom proposals, aimed at the occupied territories, and it's been quite successful.

So in the United States, some of the major church groups, like the Presbyterian Church, have taken quite a strong stand calling for complete boycott not only of, say, products from the settlements but of any institution connected with the settlements, including US multinationals – and that's an important part – that are involved in providing aid and assistance and development for the occupied territories, where everything that's going on is completely illegal of course.

The European Union has taken some steps towards boycott and divestment of the settlements. They at least have formal policies barring direct engagement with anything connected with the occupied territories. The major human rights groups like Human Rights Watch and Amnesty International have also called for strong actions directed against the settlements and occupation. And these activities I think have been substantial, successful and could be carried forward.

My own view is that, especially in the United States, but also in England, there should be efforts to try to block all military aid to Israel. In the United States, the military aid to Israel happens to be technically illegal, in violation of a law called the Leahy Law, which bans any military aid to any military units or organisations which are involved in systematic human rights abuses. And there's no question whatsoever that the IDF – the Israeli army – is involved in extreme human rights abuses in Gaza and the West Bank. So a campaign to try to press the US government to terminate military aid has I think a possible substantial basis. And, in my view, one of the faults of the popular solidarity movements, including the BDS movements, is not to press forward with this effort. Well, that's a range of, I think, quite effective BDS-style activities.

There's another strain which is directed against Israel itself. So, not attending academic conferences, boycotting Israeli universities, blocking cultural contacts and so on. In my opinion that's more dubious. For one thing, there's a strong and obvious taint of hypocrisy. So, if we're boycotting Tel Aviv University, why not boycott Harvard and Oxford, let's say, which are involved in much more serious crime? That immediately arises. And there are possible answers to that but you have to set the stage for understanding where such answers might be admissible, and the same across the board.

It has to be recognised that BDS is a tactic, it's not a policy. And tactics have to be evaluated in terms of their likely consequences. You can't say 'I just like the tactic, it makes me feel good'. You have to ask: what are the consequences of the tactic for the victims? And in general my own experience with this, and feeling about it, is that those tactical choices that have been directed against the occupation have been quite successful, whereas those directed against Israel itself have been pretty much unsuccessful. And, in fact, have also often been negative because they've elicited a backlash which is based on the kinds of considerations I just mentioned, which ended up being harmful to the Palestinian cause. Those are the questions you have to raise seriously when any tactical decision is made, whether it's BDS or civil disobedience or anything else. You have to ask yourself, primarily, what are the consequences for the victims?

QUESTIONER 7: We've been talking about a specific kind of power until now, which is governmental power. Another kind of power is the internet and social media. What is your opinion of how these platforms alter the responsibility of intellectuals? As an undergraduate student and potentially an intellectual – someday – how do we carry out our responsibilities on these platforms?

NOAM CHOMSKY: By using technologies such as the internet and social media? I think it's the same, just a different variant of the question of how we carry out our responsibilities with regard to the other kinds of privileges that come along with being what's called an intellectual.

Intellectual is kind of a strange category. It doesn't really, necessarily, correlate with your insight or understanding or anything else. But being what's called an intellectual presupposes a certain amount of privilege. Privilege confers obligations and responsibility, automatically. So those of us who are privileged enough to fall within the category of intellectuals have the responsibility to use that privilege in ways that, to go back to Martin Luther King again, 'bend the arc of history towards justice'. Well, you can do that with print media, you can do it with talks, you can do it with organising like, for example, organising the resistance organisations that I mentioned. Intellectuals played a significant part in that. The same is true of the internet and social media. You can use them constructively or they can be used harmfully. There are big struggles going on about the nature of these media right now.

A crucial question is what's called net neutrality. The internet was originally created in places like MIT, in fact, right at the lab where I was working back in the late 1950s and early 1960s, and the intention of the early engineers, scientists and others who were working on it was to create something that would be an open, free medium of interchange and expression. The internet was finally privatised in the mid 1990s, and since then it's been under substantial corporate and advertising influence, partial control. And now there's a struggle going on – primarily in the United States – as to whether to preserve or even develop further the internet as a medium of free interchange, exchange and expression of opinion, and so on, or whether to divide it, to segment it into rapid access and slow, difficult access; and of course the rapid access will be for business and power systems and so on, and the rest of it for the less privileged. And that's a major struggle going on right now in the Trump administration.

The officials who have been brought to the head of the relevant commissions in the Trump administration are opposed to net neutrality and they're trying to move towards corporate, business and government control. That's something that has to be struggled against. But for individuals, as the questioner mentioned, the choice is the usual one. How do you want to use your privilege? Do you want to use it in dedication to the needs of people who are being oppressed, who are suffering, who need help and assistance? Or do you want to use it to support your own privilege and advance it and advance the interest of those with power and wealth in the society? The usual question. It's different because these are different media, but otherwise it's the same question.

Bibliography

Achen, Christopher and Larry Bartels. 'Democracy for realists: Holding up a mirror to the electorate.' *Juncture* 22, no. 4 (2016): 269–75.

Achen, Christopher and Larry Bartels. *Democracy for Realists: Why Elections Do Not Produce Responsive Government.* Princeton, NJ: Princeton University Press, 2016.

Adelman, Paul. *Gladstone, Disraeli and Later Victorian Politics.* Harlow: Longman, 1970.

Albert, Michael. *Remembering Tomorrow: From the Politics of Opposition to What We Are For.* New York: Seven Stories Press, 2006.

Alterman, Eric. 'The professors, the press, the think tanks – and their problems.' *Bulletin of the American Association of University Professors,* May–June 2011. https://www.aaup.org/article/ professors-press-think-tanks—and-their-problems

Alternative News Collective, The. 'An open letter to President Vest.' *The Thistle* 9, no. 7. http://web.mit.edu/activities/thistle/v9/9.07/ tv9.07.html (accessed 2 April 2017).

Alternative News Collective, The. 'Who is John Deutch?' *The Thistle* 9, no. 7. http://web.mit.edu/activities/thistle/v9/9.07/tv9.07.html (accessed 2 April 2017).

American National Election Studies Guide to Public Opinion. 'Is the government run for the benefit of all 1964–2012: Response "few big interests".' http://www.electionstudies.org/nesguide/graphs/ g5a_2_1.htm (accessed July 2018).

Army Research and Development News Magazine. 'Tri-Services honor MIT achievements in military electronics research and development.' *Army Research and Development News Magazine,* 12, no. 4, July–August 1971, 68. Washington: HQ Department of the Army. https://hdl.handle.net/2027/mdp.39015078436956?urlappend =%3Bseq=242 (accessed November 2018).

Bailey, Kathleen. 'Why we have to keep the bomb.' *Bulletin of the Atomic Scientists,* January 1995, 31.

Bakshy, Eytan, Solomon Messing and Lada Adamic. 'Exposure to ideologically diverse news and opinion on Facebook.' *Science* 348, no. 6239 (2015): 1130–32.

Barsky, Robert. *Noam Chomsky: A Life of Dissent*. Cambridge, MA: MIT Press, 1997.

BBC. 'Reality Check: What is the Prevent strategy?' *BBC News*, 4 June 2017. http://www.bbc.co.uk/news/election-2017-40151991 (accessed February 2018).

Beard, Mary. 'Women in power.' *London Review of Books* 39, no. 6 (2017): 9–14.

Beinart, Peter. 'Trump's anti-Muslim political strategy.' *The Atlantic*, 29 November 2017. https://www.theatlantic.com/politics/archive/2017/11/trumps-anti-muslim-retweets-shouldnt-surprise-you/547031/ (accessed July 2018).

Belafonte, Harry and Noam Chomsky. 'The search for the rebel heart.' Interview by Amy Goodman and Juan González. *Democracy Now*, 7 December 2016. https://www.democracynow.org/2016/12/7/the_search_for_the_rebel_heart (accessed September 2018).

Bell, Daniel. *The End of Ideology: On the Exhaustion of Political Ideas in the Fifties*. New York: The Free Press, 1962.

Bender, Bryan. 'MIT team helps disarm bombs.' *The Tech* 126, no. 7, 28 February 2006, 13. http://tech.mit.edu/V126/PDF/V126-N7.pdf (accessed November 2018).

Benedictus, Leo. 'Noam Chomsky on Donald Trump: "Almost a death knell for the human species".' *The Guardian*, 20 May 2016.

Berlin, Isaiah. 'The counter-enlightenment.' In *Dictionary of the History of Ideas*, Vol II, edited by Philip P. Wiener. New York: Scribner's, 1973. Reproduced as Chapter One of *Against the Current: Essays in the History of Ideas*, edited by Henry Hardy. Oxford: Oxford University Press, 1981.

Berman, Sheri. 'Why identity politics benefits the right more than the left.' *The Guardian*, 14 July 2018. https://www.theguardian.com/commentisfree/2018/jul/14/identity-politics-right-left-trump-racism (accessed November 2018).

Bethlehem, Daniel. 'Principles relevant to the scope of a state's right to self-defense against an imminent or actual armed attack by non-state actor.' *American Journal of International Law* 106 (2012): 770–77.

Boghossian, Paul. *Fear of Knowledge: Against Relativism and Constructivism*. Oxford: Oxford University Press, 2007.

Boycott, Owen. 'Attorney general calls for new legal basis for pre-emptive military strikes.' *The Guardian*, 11 January 2017.

Brennan, Donald George. *ABM, Yes or No? Center Occasional Papers* 2, no. 2. Santa Barbara, CA: Center for the Study of Democratic Institutions, 1969.

Bridger, Sarah. *Scientists at War: The Ethics of Cold War Weapons Research.* Cambridge, MA: Harvard University Press, 2015.

Broder, David S. *Democracy Derailed: Initiative Campaigns and the Power of Money.* New York: Harcourt: 2000.

Brookes, Andrew. *Force V: The History of Britain's Airborne Deterrent.* London: Jane's, 1982.

Brown, Harold. Department of Defense Annual Report Fiscal Year 1981. https://history.defense.gov/Portals/70/Documents/annual_re ports/1981_DoD_AR.pdf?ver=2014-06-24-150845-130 (accessed November 2018).

Butler, Lee. 'Death by deterrence.' *Resurgence* 193 (March/April 1999). https://dwij.org/forum/statesperson/general_lee_butler. htm (accessed November 2018).

Chappell, Sophie. 'Political deliberation under conditions of deception: The case of Brexit.' *Think* 15 (2016): 7–13.

Chepesiuk, Ron. *Sixties Radicals, Then and Now: Candid Conversations with those who Shaped the Era.* Jefferson, NC: McFarland, 1995.

Chomsky, Daniel. 'A distorting mirror: Major media coverage of Americans' tax policy preferences.' *Institute for New Economic Thinking,* April 2018. https://www.ineteconomics.org/research/ research-papers/a-distorting-mirror-major-media-coverage-of-americans-tax-policy-preferences (accessed November 2018).

Chomsky, Noam. *Current Issues in Linguistic Theory.* The Hague: Mouton, 1964.

Chomsky, Noam. *Aspects of the Theory of Syntax.* Cambridge, MA: MIT Press, 1965.

Chomsky, Noam. *Cartesian Linguistics: A Chapter in the History of Rationalist Thought.* New York and London: Harper & Row, 1966.

Chomsky, Noam. 'Reply to critics.' *New York Review of Books,* 20 April 1967.

Chomsky, Noam. 'The responsibility of intellectuals.' *New York Review of Books,* 23 February 1967. https://chomsky.info/19670223/ (accessed November 2018).

Chomsky, Noam. '"The Responsibility of Intellectuals": An exchange.' *New York Review of Books,* 23 March 1967.

Chomsky, Noam. *Language and Mind.* New York: Harcourt, Brace and World, 1968.

Chomsky, Noam. *American Power and the New Mandarins.* New York: Pantheon, 1969.

Chomsky, Noam. 'In North Vietnam.' *New York Review of Books,* 13 August 1970.

Chomsky, Noam. 'Day at night: Noam Chomsky, author, lecturer, philosopher, and linguist.' Interview by James Day. CUNY TV, 9 April 1974. https://www.youtube.com/watch?v=rH8SicnqSC4 (accessed November 2018).

Chomsky, Noam. *The Logical Structure of Linguistic Theory*. New York: Plenum Press, 1975.

Chomsky, Noam. *Morphophonemics of Modern Hebrew*. New York: Garland, 1979.

Chomsky, Noam. *The Washington Connection and Third World Fascism*. Montréal: Black Rose Books, 1979.

Chomsky, Noam. *Towards a New Cold War: Essays on the Current Crisis and How We Got There*. Great Britain: Sinclair Browne, 1982.

Chomsky, Noam. *Language and Politics*, edited by Carlos P. Otero. Montréal: Black Rose Books, 1988.

Chomsky, Noam. *The Chomsky Reader*, edited by James Peck. London: Serpent's Tail, 1988.

Chomsky, Noam. *Necessary Illusions: Thought Control in Democratic Societies*. London: Pluto, 1989.

Chomsky, Noam. *Deterring Democracy*. London: Verso, 1991.

Chomsky, Noam. 'Language: The cognitive revolutions.' (20th Killian Award Lecture). Filmed 8 April 1992 at MIT, Cambridge, MA. https://infinitehistory.mit.edu/video/20th-killian-award-lecture%E2%80%94noam-chomsky (accessed January 2018).

Chomsky, Noam. 'Noam Chomsky – The war on unions and workers' rights.' Filmed 9 May 1995 at MIT, Cambridge, MA. https://www.youtube.com/watch?v=lhgaARgTdAk (accessed March 2018).

Chomsky, Noam. *Class Warfare: Interviews with David Barsamian*. London: Pluto Press, 1996.

Chomsky, Noam. 'What makes mainstream media mainstream.' *Z Magazine*, October 1997.

Chomsky, Noam. *The New Military Humanism: Lessons From Kosovo*. Monroe, ME: Common Courage Press, 1999.

Chomsky, Noam. *On Nature and Language*. Cambridge: Cambridge University Press, 2002.

Chomsky, Noam. *Understanding Power: The Indispensable Chomsky*, edited by Peter Mitchell and John Schoeffel. New York: The New Press, 2002.

Chomsky, Noam. *Chomsky on Democracy and Education*, edited by Carlos P. Otero. New York and London: RoutledgeFalmer, 2003.

Chomsky, Noam. *Radical Priorities*, edited by Carlos P. Otero. Oakland, CA: AK Press, 2003.

Chomsky, Noam. *Letters From Lexington: Reflections on Propaganda*, 2nd ed. London: Pluto Press, 2004.

Chomsky, Noam. *Failed States: The Abuse of Power and the Assault on Democracy*. New York: Metropolitan Books, 2006.

Chomsky, Noam. 'Infinite history project.' Interview by Karen Arenson. 29 May 2009. https://archive.org/details/NoamChomsky-Infinite HistoryProject-2009/ (accessed November 2018).

Chomsky, Noam. 'The responsibility of intellectuals, redux: Using privilege to challenge the state.' *Boston Review*, 1 September 2011. http://bostonreview.net/noam-chomsky-responsibility-of-intellec tuals-redux (accessed December 2018).

Chomsky, Noam. 'Chomsky on Snowden & why NSA surveillance doesn't stop terror while the U.S. drone war creates it.' Interview by Amy Goodman. *Democracy Now*, 3 March 2015. https://www. democracynow.org/2015/3/3/chomsky_on_snowden_why_nsa_ surveillance (accessed November 2018).

Chomsky, Noam. 'Chomsky says,' *London Review of Books* 39, no. 12 (2017). https://www.lrb.co.uk/v39/n12/letters#letter4 (accessed November 2018).

Chomsky, Noam. 'Chomsky has the last say,' *London Review of Books* 39, no. 16 (2017). https://www.lrb.co.uk/v39/n16/letters (accessed November 2018).

Chomsky, Noam. *Requiem for the American Dream: The Principles of Concentrated Wealth and Power*. New York: Seven Stories Press, 2017.

Chomsky, Noam and David Barsamian. *Chronicles of Dissent*. Stirling: AK Press, 1992.

Chomsky, Noam and David Barsamian. *Secrets, Lies, and Democracy*. Tucson, AZ: Odonian Press, 1994.

Chomsky, Noam and George Yancy. 'Noam Chomsky on the roots of American racism.' *New York Times*, 18 March 2018. https:// opinionator.blogs.nytimes.com/2015/03/18/noam-chomsky-on- the-roots-of-american-racism/ (accessed February 2018).

Chu, Jennifer. 'MIT cheetah robot lands the running jump.' *MIT News*, 29 May 2015. http://news.mit.edu/2015/cheetah-robot-lands- running-jump-0529 (accessed February 2017).

Chu, Jennifer. 'Driving drones can be a drag.' *MIT News*, 14 November 2012. http://news.mit.edu/2012/boredom-and-unmanned-aerial- vehicles-1114 (accessed February 2017).

Civicus. 'CIVICUS Monitor: Tracking Civic Space.' http://www.civicus. org/index.php/what-we-do/knowledge-analysis/civicus-monitor (accessed February 2018).

Civicus. 'Who we are.' https://www.civicus.org/index.php/who-we-are/about-civicus (accessed 28 May 2018).

Coatsworth, John. 'The Cold War in Central America, 1975–1991.' In *The Cambridge History of the Cold War*, edited by Melvyn P. Leffler and Odd Arne Westad, 201–21. Cambridge: Cambridge University Press, 2010.

Cohen, Joshua and Joel Rogers. 'Knowledge, morality and hope: The social thought of Noam Chomsky.' *New Left Review* 187 (1991): 5–27.

Corporate Legal Accountability Quarterly Bulletin, The, Issue 24, September 2017. BHRRC. https://us3.campaign-archive.com/?u=bdd1a6a40fffad39c8719632f&id=36e3109468 (accessed September 2018).

Cowan, Rich. 'Military provost.' *Science for the People*, March–April 1988.

Crozier, Michel, Samuel Huntington and Joji Watanuki. *The Crisis of Democracy: Report on the Governability of Democracies to the Trilateral Commission*. New York: New York University Press, 1975.

Darwish, Adel and Gregory Alexander. *Unholy Babylon: The Secret History of Saddam's War*. London: Gollancz, 1991.

Debons, Anthony. 'Command and control: Technology and social impact.' *Advances in Computers*, 11 (1971): 319–90. New York: Academic Press.

Deutch, John. 'Myth and reality in chemical warfare.' *Chemical and Engineering News* 60, no. 1, February 1982. http://web.mit.edu/chemistry/deutch/policy/1982-MythRealityChemWarfare-CEN.pdf

Deutch, John. 'The decision to modernize US intercontinental ballistic missiles.' *Science* 244, no. 4911 (1989): 1445–50.

Economist, The. 'Berned out.' *The Economist*, 7 June 2018. https://www.economist.com/united-states/2018/06/07/berned-out (accessed November 2018).

Edwards, Kari and Edward Smith. 'A disconfirmation bias in the evaluation of arguments.' *Journal of Personality and Social Psychology* 71, no. 1 (1996): 5–24.

Ellsberg, Daniel. 'Call to mutiny.' In *Protest and Survive*, edited by Edward Thompson and Dan Smith, i–xxviii. New York and London: Monthly Review Press, 1981.

Ellsberg, Daniel. *The Doomsday Machine: Confessions of a Nuclear War Planner*. New York: Bloomsbury, 2017.

Facchini, Giovanni, Yotam Margalit and Hiroyuki Nakata. 'Countering public opposition to immigration: The impact of information campaigns.' *IZA Institute of Labor Economics Discussion Paper Series* 10420 (December 2016). http://ftp.iza.org/dp10420.pdf

Feldman, Bob. 'Columbia University's IDA Jason Project 1960s work – Part 9.' 1 April 2008. http://bfeldman68.blogspot.co.uk/2008/04/columbia-universitys-ida-jason-project.html (accessed December 2016).

Ferguson, Thomas. *Golden Rule: The Investment Theory of Party Competition and the Logic of Money-Driven Political Systems.* Chicago: University of Chicago Press, 1995.

Fernandes, Clinton. *The Independence of East Timor: Multi-Dimensional Perspectives – Occupation, Resistance, and International Political Activism.* Brighton: Sussex Academic Press, 2011.

Finkbeiner, Anne. *The Jasons: The Secret History of Science's Postwar Elite.* New York: Penguin, 2007.

Fleming, Sam. 'Battle lines: The fight for a fair vote in America.' *The Financial Times*, 2 August 2018.

Friedersdorf, Conor. 'What James Clapper doesn't understand about Edward Snowden.' *The Atlantic*, 24 February 2014. https://www.theatlantic.com/politics/archive/2014/02/what-james-clapper-doesnt-understand-about-edward-snowden/284032/ (accessed February 2018).

Friel, Howard. *Chomsky and Dershowitz: On Endless War and the End of Civil Liberties.* Northampton, MA: Interlink Books, 2013.

Garfinkel, Simson. 'Building 20, a survey.' No date. http://ic.media.mit.edu/projects/JBW/ARTICLES/SIMSONG.HTM (accessed January 2017).

Gigerenzer, Gerd. 'Striking a blow for sanity in theories of rationality.' In *Models of a Man: Essays in Memory of Herbert A. Simon*, edited by Maxime Augier and James March, 389–409. Cambridge, MA: MIT Press, 2004.

Gigerenzer, Gerd. 'Why heuristics work.' *Perspectives on Psychological Science* 3, no. 1 (2008): 20–29.

Gilens, Martin. *Affluence and Influence: Economic Inequality and Political Power in America.* Princeton, NJ: Princeton University Press, 2012.

Glenn, Daniel J. 'A crack in the dome – Twenty years later, MIT still doing military research projects.' *The Tech* 109, no. 6, 24 February 1989, 5. https://thetech.com/issues/109/6 (accessed November 2018).

Glenza, Jessica. 'Disgraced anti-vaxxer Andrew Wakefield aims to advance his agenda in Texas election.' *The Guardian*, 26 February 2018. https://www.theguardian.com/us-news/2018/

feb/26/texas-vaccinations-safety-andrew-wakefield-fear-elections (accessed 28 May 2018).

Green, Bert. *Digital Computers in Research: An Introduction for Behavioral and Social Scientists*. New York: McGraw-Hill, 1963.

Green, Bert, Carol Chomsky, Kenneth Laughery and Alice Wolf, *The Baseball Program: An Automatic Question-Answerer, Vol. 1*. Bedford, MA: MIT Lincoln Laboratory, 1963.

Grigorieff, Alexis, Christopher Roth and Diego Ubfal. 'Does information change attitudes towards immigrants? Representative evidence from survey experiments.' *IZA Institute of Labor Economics, Discussion Paper series*, no. 10419 (December 2016). http://ftp.iza.org/dp10419.pdf

Hamilton, Andrew. 'M.I.T.: March 4 revisited amid political turmoil.' *Science*, 3924, 13 March 1970.

Harris, Abram L. 'John Stuart Mill: Servant of the East India Company.' *The Canadian Journal of Economics and Political Science/ Revue Canadienne d'Economique et de Science Politique* 30, no. 2 (1964), 185–202.

Heinze, Eric. 'Ten arguments for – and against – "no-platforming".' Last modified 28 March 2016. http://freespeechdebate.com/discuss/ten-arguments-for-and-against-no-platforming/ (accessed October 2018).

Herman, Edward S. 'The propaganda model: A retrospective.' *Against All Reason*, 1, 2003, 1–14.

Herman, Edward S. and Noam Chomsky. *Manufacturing Consent: The Political Economy of the Mass Media*. New York: Pantheon Books, 1988.

Herman, Edward S. and Noam Chomsky. 'Propaganda mill: The media churn out the "official line".' *The Progressive*, June 1988: 14–15.

Hewlett, Richard and Francis Duncan. *Atomic Shield: A History of the United States Atomic Energy Commission, Vol. 2, 1947/1952*. Washington: AEC, 1972.

Huang, Thomas T. 'Examining John Deutch's Pentagon connections.' *The Tech* 108, no. 26, 27 May 1988, 2 and 11. https://thetech.com/issues/108/26 (accessed November 2018).

Independent, The. 'Hypocrisy and the nuclear deterrent.' *The Independent*, 2 May 2005.

International Human Rights and Conflict Resolution Clinic at Stanford Law School and Global Justice Clinic at NYU School of Law. 'Living under drones: Death, injury and trauma to civilians from US drone practices in Pakistan.' 2012. https://www-cdn.law.stanford.

edu/wp-content/uploads/2015/07/Stanford-NYU-Living-Under-Drones.pdf (accessed November 2018).

Ippolito, Thomas. 'Effects of variation of uranium enrichment on nuclear submarine reactor design.' MSc thesis, MIT, 1990.

Jenkins, Simon. 'This £100bn. armageddon weapon won't make us one jot safer.' *The Guardian*, 25 September 2013.

Johnson, Loch. *Secret Agencies: U.S. Intelligence in a Hostile World.* New Haven and London: Yale University Press, 1998.

Jones, Owen. *Chavs: The Demonization of the Working Class.* London: Verso, 2011.

Kahneman, Daniel. *Thinking, Fast and Slow.* New York: Farrar, Straus and Giroux, 2011.

Kahneman, Daniel and Amos Tversky. 'On the psychology of prediction.' *Psychological Review* 80, no. 4 (1973): 237–51.

Kay, Lily. *Who Wrote the Book of Life? A History of the Genetic Code.* Stanford, CA: Stanford University Press, 2000.

Keller, Bill. 'Pentagon panel said to support building of small mobile missile.' *New York Times*, 2 February 1986.

Keyser, Samuel Jay. 'Our manner of speaking.' *Technology Review*, February 1964.

Keyser, Samuel Jay. 'Linguistic theory and system design.' In *Information System Sciences*, edited by Joseph Spiegel and Donald Walker, 495–505. Washington, DC: MITRE Corp., 1965.

Kirzinger, Ashley, Bryan Wu and Mollyann Brodie. 'Kaiser Health tracking poll – March 2018: Views on prescription drug pricing and Medicare-for-all proposals.' KFF: Henry J Kaiser Family Foundation, 23 March 2018. https://www.kff.org/health-reform/poll-finding/kaiser-health-tracking-poll-March-2018-prescription-drug-pricing-medicare-for-all-proposals/ (accessed November 2018).

Kissinger, Henry. *American Foreign Policy: Three Essays.* New York: Norton, 1969.

Knight, Chris. 'Chomsky's students recall their time at the MITRE Corporation.' 18 February 2018. http://scienceandrevolution.org/blog/2018/2/17/chomskys-students-recall-their-time-at-the-mitre-corporation (accessed May 2018).

Knight, Chris. 'Noam Chomsky's "The Responsibility of Intellectuals", 50 years on – Video of conference at University College London,' Science And Revolution, 25 February 2017. http://scienceandrevolution.org/blog/noam-chomskys-the-responsibility-of-intellectuals-50-years-on (accessed October 2018).

Knight, Chris. *Decoding Chomsky: Science and Revolutionary Politics.* London and New Haven: Yale University Press, 2016.

Koerner, Konrad and Matsuji Tajima. *Noam Chomsky: A Personal Bibliography, 1951–1986.* Amsterdam/Philadelphia: John Benjamins, 1986.

Krugman, Paul. 'The new political correctness.' *New York Times* blog post, 26 May 2012. https://krugman.blogs.nytimes.com/2012/05/26/the-new-political-correctness/ (accessed 28 May 2018).

Lau, Ryanne. 'Social media as tool for meaningful political activism.' *McGill Left Review*, 9 March 2017. http://mcgillleftreview.com/article/social-media-tool-meaningful-political-activism (accessed 28 May 2018).

Lee, David. *Eastward: A History of the RAF in the Far East, 1945–72.* London: HMSO, 1984.

Leo, Alan. 'The soldier of tomorrow.' *MIT Technology Review*, 20 March 2002. https://www.technologyreview.com/s/401391/the-soldier-of-tomorrow/ (accessed November 2018).

Lewis, Anthony. 'Look on my works…' *New York Times*, 1 May 1975. https://www.nytimes.com/1975/05/01/archives/look-on-my-works.html (accessed November 2018).

Lewis, Anthony. 'Ghosts.' *New York Times*, 27 December 1979. https://www.nytimes.com/1979/12/27/archives/abroad-at-home-ghosts.html (accessed November 2018).

Liese, Debra. 'What do sharks have to do with democracy? Christopher Achen & Larry Bartels explain.' Princeton University Press blog, 31 March 2016. http://blog.press.princeton.edu/2016/03/31/what-do-sharks-have-to-do-with-democracy-christopher-achen-larry-bartels-explain/ (accessed February 2018).

Lightman, Alan. 'The role of the public intellectual: Remarks presented to the MIT Communications Forum "Public Intellectuals and the Academy".' 2 December 1999. http://www.mit.edu/~saleem/ivory/epil.htm (accessed September 2018).

Lodge, Milton and Charles Taber. 'Three steps toward a theory of motivated political reasoning.' In *Elements of Reason: Cognition, Choice, and the Bounds of Rationality*, edited by Arthur Lupia, Matthew McCubbins and Samuel Popkin, 183–213. Cambridge: Cambridge University Press, 2000.

Lopez, German. 'Research says there are ways to reduce racial bias. Calling people racist isn't one of them.' *Vox*, 14 August 2017. https://www.vox.com/identities/2016/11/15/13595508/racism-trump-research-study (accessed November 2018).

Macdonald, Dwight. *The Responsibility of Peoples and Other Essays in Political Criticism*. London: Gollancz, 1957.

Maduz, Linda. 'Direct democracy.' *Living Reviews in Democracy* 2, 2010. https://www.lrd.ethz.ch/index.php/lrd/issue/view/2010 (accessed November 2018).

Major, Brenda, Alison Blodorn and Gregory Major Blascovich. 'The threat of increasing diversity: Why many White Americans support Trump in the 2016 presidential election.' *Group Processes & Intergroup Relations* 21, no. 6 (2016), 861–73. Published online 20 October 2016. http://journals.sagepub.com/doi/abs/10.1177/1368430216677304

March, Eric. 'USA CEO Of Penzeys Spices achieves sales surge by standing up against discriminatory rhetoric.' Business and Human Rights Resources Centre, 20 December 2016. https://www.business-humanrights.org/en/usa-ceo-of-penzeys-spices-achieves-sales-surge-by-standing-up-against-discriminatory-rhetoric (accessed February 2018).

Mares, Isabela. 'A discussion of Christopher H. Achen and Larry M. Bartels' *Democracy for Realists: Why Elections Do Not Produce Responsive Government.' Perspectives on Politics* 15, no. 1 (2017): 159–60.

Mazzarella, Diana, Emmanuel Trouche, Hugo Mercier and Ira Noveck. 'Believing what you're told: Politeness and scalar inferences.' *Frontiers of Psychology* 9 (2018): 15–27.

Mazzarella, Diana, Robert Reinecke, Ira Noveck and Hugo Mercier. 'Saying, presupposing and implicating: How pragmatics modulates commitment,' *Journal of Pragmatics* 133 (2018).

McNutt, Mike. 'Vice-president resigns: McCormack to head Comsat.' *The Tech* 85, no. 20, 20 October 1965. https://thetech.com/issues/85/20 (accessed November 2018).

McRaney, David. 'The backfire effect.' You Are Not So Smart website, 10 June 2011. https://youarenotsosmart.com/2011/06/10/the-backfire-effect/ (accessed February 2018).

Meisel, Robert and John Jacobs. *MITRE: The First Twenty Years, A History of the MITRE Corporation (1958–1978)*. Bedford, MA: MITRE Corp., 1979.

Mercier, Hugo and Dan Sperber. 'Why do humans reason? Arguments for an argumentative theory.' *Behavioral and Brain Sciences* 34, no. 2 (2011): 57–74.

Ministry Of Defence. *Statement on Defence 1963*. London: HMSO, 1963.

Ministry Of Defence. *Statement on the Defence Estimates 1995: Stable Forces in a Strong Britain.* London: HMSO, 1995.

Ministry Of Defence. '2010 to 2015 government policy: UK nuclear deterrent.' Last modified 8 May 2015. https://www.gov.uk/gov ernment/publications/2010-to-2015-government-policy-uk-nucle ar-deterrent/2010-to-2015-government-policy-uk-nuclear-deterre nt (accessed November 2018).

Minton, Anna. *Big Capital: Who is London For?* London: Penguin, 2017.

MIT News. 'Ocean engineering students set stage for a smarter fleet.' *MIT News,* 14 August 2013. http://news.mit.edu/2013/ocean-engi neering-students-set-stage-for-a-smarter-fleet (accessed February 2017).

Morgan, Gary and Bencie Woll. *Directions in Sign Language Acquisition.* Amsterdam: John Benjamins, 2002.

Morning Consult and Politico. 'National tracking poll #170911: Crosstabulation results.' *Morning Consult,* 14–17 September 2017. https://morningconsult.com/wp-content/uploads/2017/09/170 911_crosstabs_Politico_LIM_v1_AP-1.pdf (accessed November 2018).

Nabulsi, Karma. 'Don't go to the Doctor.' *London Review of Books* 39, no. 10 (2016): 27–8.

Nagel, Thomas. *The Last Word.* Oxford: Oxford University Press, 1997.

New York Times. 'A secret seminar.' *New York Times,* 2 July 1971. https:// www.nytimes.com/1971/07/02/archives/a-secret-seminar.html (accessed November 2018).

Nichols, Tom. *The Death of Expertise: The Campaign Against Established Knowledge and Why It Matters.* Oxford: Oxford University Press, 2016.

Nisbett, Richard and Timothy Wilson. 'Telling more than we can know: Verbal reports on mental processes.' *Psychological Review* 84, no. 3 (1977): 231–59.

Nygreen, Ted. 'Vietnam demonstrations, students join protests.' *The Tech* 85, no. 20, 20 October 1965. https://thetech.com/issues/85/20 (accessed November 2018).

Nyhan, Brendan and Jason Reifler. 'When corrections fail: The persistence of political misperceptions.' *Political Behavior* 32, no. 2 (2010): 303–30.

O'Connell, Mary Ellen. 'Unlawful killing with combat drones: A case study of Pakistan, 2004–2009.' *Notre Dame Law School, Legal Studies Research Paper* 09-43 (2010): 13. https://papers.ssrn.com/sol3/ papers.cfm?abstract_id=1501144 (accessed November 2018).

O'Neill, Kathryn. 'Scientific reunion commemorates 50 years of linguistics at MIT.' Report on meeting held 9–11 December 2011. MIT Linguistics website. https://shass.mit.edu/news/news-2011-scientific-reunion-commemorates-50-years-linguistics-mit (accessed November 2018).

Orwell, George. 'The freedom of the press.' (Written as introduction to *Animal Farm* c. 1945.) https://www.bl.uk/collection-items/orwells-proposed-introduction-to-animal-farm (accessed July 2018).

Parini, Jay. 'Noam Chomsky's "Responsibility of Intellectuals" after 50 years: It's an even heavier responsibility now.' *Salon*, 11 February 2017.

Platt, Tony. *Beyond These Walls: Rethinking Crime and Punishment in the United States.* New York: St Martin's Press, 2019.

Porter, Bernard. 'Schooled in anarchy.' *Times Literary Supplement*, 6 January 2012. https://www.the-tls.co.uk/articles/private/schooled-in-anarchy/ (accessed November 2018).

Powell, Jr., Lewis F. 'Confidential memorandum: Attack of American free enterprise system.' 23 August 1971. Available online at http://reclaimdemocracy.org/powell_memo_lewis/ (accessed 19 October 2018).

Power, Samantha. *A Problem From Hell: America and the Age of Genocide.* New York: Basic Books, 2002.

Power, Samantha. 'The everything explainer.' *New York Times*, 4 January 2004. https://www.nytimes.com/2004/01/04/books/the-everything-explainer.html (accessed November 2018).

Powers, Thomas. 'Computer security; The whiz kids versus the old boys.' *New York Times Magazine*, 3 December 2000. https://www.nytimes.com/2000/12/03/magazine/computer-security-the-whiz-kid-vs-Civettini-old-boys.html (accessed November 2018).

Prato, Carlo and Bruno Strulovici. 'The hidden cost of direct democracy: How ballot initiatives affect politicians' selection and incentives.' *Journal of Theoretical Politics* 29, no. 3 (2017): 440–66.

Priest, Andrew. *Kennedy, Johnson and NATO: Britain, America and the Dynamics of Alliance, 1962–68.* London and New York: Routledge, 2006.

Rai, Milan. *Chomsky's Politics.* London and New York: Verso, 1995.

Redlawsk, David P. 'Hot cognition or cool consideration? Testing the effects of motivated reasoning on political decision making.' *The Journal of Politics* 64, no. 4 (2002): 1021–44

Redlawsk, David P., Andrew J. W. Civettini and Karen M. Emmerson. 'The affective tipping point: Do motivated reasoners ever "get it"?' *Political Psychology* 31, no. 4 (2010): 563–93.

Rhodes, Richard. *Dark Sun: The Making of the Hydrogen Bomb*. New York: Simon & Schuster, 1995.

Rhodes, Tom. 'Britain kept secret nuclear weapons in Singapore and Cyprus.' *Sunday Times*, 31 December 2000.

Rich, Nathaniel and George Steinmetz. 'Losing earth: The decade we almost stopped climate change.' *New York Times*, 1 August 2018. https://www.nytimes.com/interactive/2018/08/01/magazine/climate-change-losing-earth.html (accessed November 2018).

Rifkind, Malcolm. 'UK defence strategy: A continuing role for nuclear weapons?' In *Brassey's Defence Yearbook 1994*. London: Brassey's, 1994.

Roberts, Neil. 'A discussion of Christopher H. Achen and Larry M. Bartels' *Democracy for Realists: Why Elections Do Not Produce Responsive Government*.' *Perspectives on Politics* 15, no. 1 (2017): 154–6.

Robinson, Dan. 'Profiles in research: Interview with Bert F. Green.' *Journal of Educational and Behavioral Statistics* 29, no. 2 (2004): 261–8.

Rosenblith, Walter (ed.). *Jerry Wiesner: Scientist, Statesman, Humanist: Memories and Memoirs*. Cambridge, MA: MIT Press, 2003.

Rubio, Antonio. 'El Estado Mayor de El Salvador ordenó "eliminar" a Ignacio Ellacuría.' *El Mundo* (Spain), 22 November 2009. http://www.elmundo.es/elmundo/2009/11/21/espana/1258830475.html (accessed November 2018).

Rutledge, Pamela B. 'Four ways social media is redefining activism.' *Psychology Today blog*, 6 October 2010. https://www.psychologytoday.com/gb/blog/positively-media/201010/four-ways-social-media-is-redefining-activism (accessed 28 May 2018).

Sabl, Andrew. 'A discussion of Christopher H. Achen and Larry M. Bartels' *Democracy for Realists: Why Elections Do Not Produce Responsive Government*.' *Perspectives on Politics* 15, no. 1 (2017): 157–8.

Said, Edward. *Humanism and Democratic Criticism*. New York: Columbia University Press, 2004.

Schalk, David. *War and the Ivory Tower: Algeria and Vietnam*. Oxford: Oxford University Press, 1991.

Schwartz, Nelson D. and Ben Casselman. 'Workers hardest hit by recession are joining in recovery.' *New York Times*, 3 August 2018. https://www.nytimes.com/2018/08/03/business/economy/july-jobs-report-2018.html (accessed November 2018).

Schwennicke, Antje. 'A discussion of Christopher H. Achen and Larry M. Bartels' *Democracy for Realists: Why Elections Do Not Produce Responsive Government.' Perspectives on Politics* 15, no. 1 (2017): 148–51.

Scowcroft, Brent. *Report of the President's Commission on Strategic Forces.* Washington, DC: The White House, 1983.

Scowcroft, Brent, John Deutch and James Woolsey. 'A small, survivable, mobile ICBM.' *Washington Post*, 26 December 1986.

Sengupta, Kim. 'Hoon warns rogue states to expect nuclear retaliation.' *The Independent*, 21 March 2002.

Siddiqui, Faiz. 'Uber triggers protest for not supporting taxi strike against refugee ban.' *Washington Post*, 29 January 2017. https://www. washingtonpost.com/news/dr-gridlock/wp/2017/01/29/uber-triggers-protest-for-not-supporting-taxi-strike-against-refugee-ban/ (accessed February 2018).

Smith, Neil and Nicholas Allott. *Chomsky: Ideas and Ideals*, 3rd ed. Cambridge: Cambridge University Press, 2016.

Snead, David. *The Gaither Committee, Eisenhower, and the Cold War.* Columbus, OH: Ohio State University Press, 1999.

Spectator, The. 'Margaret Thatcher in quotes.' *The Spectator*, 8 April 2013. https://blogs.spectator.co.uk/2013/04/margaret-thatcher-in-quotes/ (accessed November 2018).

STRATCOM. *Essentials of Post-Cold War Deterrence*, 1995. http://www.nukestrat.com/us/stratcom/SAGessentials.PDF (accessed November 2018).

Taber, Charles S. and Milton Lodge. 'Motivated skepticism in the evaluation of political beliefs.' *American Journal of Political Science* 3, no. 50 (2006): 755–69.

Tech, The. 'McCormack, new vice-president, is a man of great distinction.' *The Tech* 77, no. 29, 4 October 1957: 1. https://thetech.com/issues/77/29 (accessed November 2018).

Tech, The. 'Course 21 offers two new subjects.' *The Tech* 85, no. 17, 29 September 1965: 1. https://thetech.com/issues/85/17 (accessed November 2018).

Tech, The. 'Committee to meet, plan participation in Viet Nam protests.' *The Tech* 85, no. 17, 29 September 1965: 11. https://thetech.com/issues/85/17 (accessed November 2018).

Tech, The. 'Chomsky accepts post; Ward Professor named.' *The Tech* 86, no. 20, 22 April 1966. https://thetech.com/issues/86/20 (accessed November 2018).

Technology Review. 'MIT and social responsibility.' *Technology Review*, June 1970, 82.

Thompson, William. *At the Edge of History*. New York: Harper and Row, 1971.

Turse, Nick. *Kill Anything that Moves: The Real American War in Vietnam*. New York: Picador, 2013.

UCL. 'UCL marks a place in British intellectual history for John Stuart Mill.' Press release, 23 March 2006. https://www.ucl.ac.uk/media/library/mill (accessed September 2018).

United Press International. 'MIT students allege defense conflict.' 2 June 1989. https://www.upi.com/Archives/1989/06/02/MIT-students-allege-defense-conflict/2508612763200/ (accessed February 2017).

US Department of Defense. 'Department of Defense announces successful micro-drone demonstration.' Press release, 9 January 2017. https://www.defense.gov/News/News-Releases/News-Release-View/Article/1044811/department-of-defense-announces-successful-micro-drone-demonstration/ (accessed November 2018).

Vedantham, Anu. 'Teach-in focuses on research and activism.' *The Tech* 109, no. 9, 7 March 1989, 2. https://thetech.com/issues/109/9 (accessed November 2018).

Verrier, Anthony. *Through the Looking Glass: British Foreign Policy in an Age of Illusions*. London: Jonathan Cape, 1983.

Versi, Miqdaad. 'Prevent is failing. Any effective strategy must include Muslim communities.' *The Guardian*, 20 October 2016. https://www.theguardian.com/commentisfree/2016/oct/20/prevent-isnt-working-inclusive-muslim-communities-counter-terrorism (accessed 4 November 2018).

Wallerstein, Immanuel and Paul Starr, eds. *The University Crisis Reader*. New York: Random House, 1972.

Weiner, Tim. 'The C.I.A.'s most important mission: itself.' *New York Times*, 10 December 1995. https://www.nytimes.com/1995/12/10/magazine/the-cia-s-most-important-mission-itself.html (accessed November 2018).

Wiesner, Jerome. *Report to the President-Elect of the Ad Hoc Committee on Space*. 10 January 1961. www.hq.nasa.gov/office/pao/History/report61.html (accessed September 2016).

Wiesner, Jerome. 'A successful experiment.' *Naval Research Reviews* 21, no. 7 (July 1966).

Wiesner, Jerome. 'Prof. Wiesner explains.' *Chicago Tribune*, 29 June 1969, 24. http://scienceandrevolution.org/blog/2018/1/14/

chomskys-supervisors-at-mit-wiesner-and-mccormack   (accessed
November 2018).

Wiesner, Jerome. 'War and peace in the nuclear age; bigger bang for the
buck, a; interview with Jerome Wiesner, 1986 [1].' WGBH Media
Library and Archives. 27 March 1986. http://openvault.wgbh.org/
catalog/V_DD3A084107E94632B6AD7D428A966304   (accessed
March 2017).

Wiesner, Jerome. *Jerry Wiesner: Scientist, Statesman, Humanist: Memories
and Memoirs.* Cambridge, MA: MIT Press, 2003.

Wigert, Jon. 'Profile: General Mac.' *The Tech* 78, no. 36, 21 October 1958,
2. https://thetech.com/issues/78/36 (accessed November 2018).

Wikipedia, 'Mike Mansfield'. https://en.wikipedia.org/wiki/Mike_
Mansfield#Mansfield_Amendments (accessed November 2018).

Wilkin, Peter. *Noam Chomsky: On Power, Knowledge and Human Nature.*
London: Macmillan Press, 1997.

Wilson, Jon. *India Conquered: Britain's Raj and the Chaos of Empire.*
London: Simon & Schuster, 2016.

Wright, Gerald. 'A discussion of Christopher H. Achen and Larry M. Bartels'
*Democracy for Realists: Why Elections Do Not Produce Responsive
Government.' Perspectives on Politics* 15, no. 1 (2017): 161–2.

Wubbena, Zane. 'Breathing secondhand smoke: Gatekeeping for "good
education", passive democracy, and the mass media. An interview
with Noam Chomsky.' *Critical Education* 6, no. 8 (2015): 1–8.

Yaqoob, Waseem. 'Why we strike.' *London Review of Books,* 16 February
2018. https://www.lrb.co.uk/blog/2018/02/16/w-yaqoobgmail-
com/why-we-strike/ (accessed September 2018).

Zingales, Luigi. 'Towards a political theory of the firm.' *Journal of
Economic Perspectives* 31, no. 3 (2017): 113–30.

Zwicky, Arnold. 'Grammars of number theory: Some examples.' Working
Paper W-6671. Bedford, MA: The MITRE Corporation, 1963.
https://web.stanford.edu/~zwicky/grammars-of-number-theory.
pdf (accessed February 2018).

Zwicky, Arnold and Stephen Isard. 'Some aspects of tree theory.' Working
Paper W-6674. Bedford, MA: The MITRE Corporation, 1963.
https://web.stanford.edu/~zwicky/some-aspects-of-tree-theory.
pdf (accessed February 2018).

Zwicky, Arnold, Joyce Friedman, Barbara C. Hall (Partee) and Donald
Walker. 'The MITRE syntactic analysis procedure for transformational grammars.' *AFIPS Conference Proceedings: Fall Joint Computer
Conference* (1965), 317–26. https://web.stanford.edu/~zwicky/
mitre-syntactic-analysis-procedure.pdf (accessed February 2018).

Index

Index note: Page numbers in *italic* refer to images. Page numbers in the form 41n12 refer to endnotes.

academia 9–10, 17, 27, 29, 72, 90
academic freedom 9, 72
Achen, Christopher 33, 34–5, 36, 37, 38–9, 40, 41n12
activism
    Chomsky commentaries 81, 86, 89–90, 94–6
    ROI reflections 13, 19, 30, 60, 63
    UCL conference Q&A 103, 108
affirmative action 35
Albert, Michael 57–8
Allott, Nicholas
    Chomsky commentary on 81–4
    on ROI 1–4, 32–44
    UCL conference x in 3
Alterman, Eric 17
American Power and the New Mandarins
    (Chomsky) x, 60–1
Americas, conquest of 88–9, 107–8
Amnesty International 118
anti-intellectualism 14–16, 24n29
anti-miscegenation 89
anti-racism 28
antisemitism 28, 29
anti-war movement
    Chomsky commentaries 87, 89, 91, 95, 97
    Chomsky on historical context of ROI x, 5–6
    Knight on ROI 60–3, 68n24
    UCL conference Q&A 109, 114
Arab Spring 19
Austria 111
autism 16, 24n32
Avnery, Uri 117

backfire effect 17, 33, 35–6, 37, 40–1, 81
BAFGOPI (Boston Area Faculty Group on
    Public Issues) 94–5
Bar-Hillel, Yehoshua 54, 95
Bartels, Larry 33, 34–5, 37, 38–9, 40, 41n12
BBC (British Broadcasting Corporation) 72
BDS movement (Boycott, Divestment,
    Sanctions) 117, 118, 119
Beard, Mary 18
Bell, Daniel 17, 21, 25n41
Bethlehem, Daniel 73–4, 88
biological warfare 48, 56, 97
black activism 9, 19, 26, 28–30, 108, 111

Black Lives Matter 19
Blair, Tony 111
Boghossian, Paul 13, 14
Boston Area Faculty Group on Public Issues
    (BAFGOPI) 94–5
The Boston Globe 6, 109
bounded rationality 37–8, 42n22
Bourne, Randolph 103
Breitbart News 11
Brexit referendum 7, 11, 14, 27
Britain
    and Americas 107–8
    and India 3, 72, 107
    nuclear weapons 46–51, 67n10, 84
    politics 18, 20, 28–9, 109–10
British Empire 4n7, 49
Broder, David 35
Brookes, Andrew 48–9
Brown, Harold 85
Bundy, McGeorge 5, 78
Business and Human Rights Resource Centre
    (BHRRC) 12
Butler, General Lee 85–6

campaign finance 39, 84, 109
Carter, Jimmy 76, 85
CELAC (The Community of Latin American
    and Caribbean States) 117
Center for Communication Studies 58
Central America 87–8, 116
A Century of Dishonor (Jackson) 89
Chappell, Sophie 11
chemical weapons 48, 56
Chicago Council 80
China 21, 106, 107
Chomsky, Carol 59
Chomsky, Noam
    Allott on ROI 1–4, 32–44
    on Allott 81–4
    American Power and the New Mandarins x,
        60–1
    commentaries x–xi, 75–101
    on historical context of ROI x–xi, 5–6
    Knight on ROI 53–70, 99
    on Knight 90–9
    Murray on ROI 71–4

on Murray 86–90
Rai on ROI 45–52
on Rai 84–6
Requiem for the American Dream 19
Smith and Smith on ROI 7–25
on Smith and Smith 76–80
UCL conference Q&A xi, 102–20
Walker on ROI 26–31
on Walker 29, 75
see also 'The Responsibility of Intellectuals'
    (ROI)
Chomsky, Valéria Wasserman xi
Chomsky, Carol 59
Churchill, Winston 10
CIA (Central Intelligence Agency) 56, 57, 63,
    66
Civettini, Andrew 36, 40
civic space 19–20
Civicus 19, 20, 25n50
civil rights 13, 23n14
class 18, 21, 23n9
climate change 18, 21, 104–6
Clinton, Bill 56, 81, 85, 110, 111
Cobden, Richard 107
Cold War 46, 53, 57, 84, 85
colonisation 88–9, 107–8
command and control 58, 59, 61, 69, 84, 91,
    93, 97
computer language 58–9, 68n31, 95
Conner, Alana 41
COP22 conference 105
Corbyn, Jeremy 28, 73, 84
counterinsurgency 116
The Crisis of Democracy (Trilateral Commission
    report) 76, 90
Cuba 2, 116, 117

Darfur 105
Deaf community 16, 24n36
Debons, Anthony 59
Debs, Eugene 103, 114
defeatism 10
democracy 17, 33–4, 39–40, 41n11, 76–7, 90,
    94, 108
Democracy for Realists (Achen and Bartels)
    34–5, 36
Democratic Party 82, 109
Deutch, John 53, 56–8, *66*, 68, 97, 101n37,
    114
Dewey, John 102–3
DiEM25 movement 84, 112
direct democracy 34, 41n11
disconfirmation bias 35
dissident intellectuals 78, 79, 103, 113
Doomsday Clock 86
Doomsday Machine (Ellsberg) 84
Down syndrome 16

Draper Lab (I-Lab) 96, 115
Dreyfus trial 78, 102
drone strikes 73–4, 88, 100n24

East India Company 3, 107
East Timor 81, 100n11
education 8, 38–9
Edwards, Kari 35
Einstein, Albert 10
election campaigns 39, 84, 109
elites 10, 38–9, 78
Ellsberg, Daniel 47, 84
El Salvador 79
Emmerson, Karen 36, 40
Engels, Friedrich 36
England 106–8 see also Britain
environmental policy 13, 104–5
eugenics 16
Europe 108, 111, 112, 118
experts 1, 14–16, 24n29, 76

Facchini, Giovanni 41
Facebook 16, 17
fake news 17
Fall, Bernard 87
false consciousness 36
Ferguson, Niall 72
Ferguson, Thomas 39
First World War 102–3, 114
folk theory of democracy 34, 42n24
Foucault, Michel 13
France 111
free press 45
'free speech' debate 24n27
Frost, David 48

genetic engineering 15, 16
genocide 26, 100n11, 108
George III, King 107
Germany 111
Gladstone, William 73
global warming 86, 104
Gove, Michael 14, 15, 24n29
grammar 92
Gramsci, Antonio 13, 32, 84, 86
Green, Bert 59
Greenspan, Alan 83
gun control 35
Gush Shalom 117

Haldeman, HR 85
Hale, Kenneth 95
Halle, Morris 95
healthcare 39
Heineken, Alfred 19
Herman, Edward 38, 45, 50, 100n19
Hitler, Adolf 78, 106, 111

Hoon, Geoff 48
housing policy 18
human rights 11, 12, 19–20, 118
Human Rights Watch 118
Hume, David 11, 23n11
Huntington, Samuel 77

identity politics 14
ideology 21, 25n41
I-Lab (Draper Lab) 96, 115
illegality 21
immigration 12, 40–1, 110
India 3, 4n7, 107, 110, 111, 112
Indonesia 48, 49
inequality 18, 71
intellectuals
    Allott on ROI 1, 2, 32
    Chomsky commentaries 7, 75, 76, 81, 90
    Chomsky on historical context of ROI 5
    intellectual confidence 9–10
    intellectual courage 9
    Murray on ROI 72–3
    public intellectuals 72–3
    Smith and Smith on ROI 8–10, 14–16, 18,
        21
    UCL conference Q&A 102, 103, 112, 113,
        119
    Walker on ROI 27, 30–1
International Monetary Fund 116
internet 16, 110, 119–20
intervention 106-7
Iraq 36, 47, 48, 49, 73, 88
ISIS 27
Islamophobia 12, 28
Israel 27, 29, 116, 117, 118

Jackson, Helen Hunt 89
Jakobson, Roman 95
Japan 106
Jefferson, Thomas 107
Jenkins, Simon 46
Jewish history 29
Johnson, Lyndon 5, 53, 64, 114

Kennedy, John F. 2, 5, 54, 55, 67n10, 87, 88,
    97, 98, 116
Keyser, Colonel Samuel Jay 68n31, 69, 94,
    101n32
King, Martin Luther 112, 119
Kissinger, Henry 2, 76
Knight, Chris
    Chomsky commentary on 90–9
    response to Chomsky 99
    on ROI 53–70
    UCL conference Q&A xin 3, 102, 104, 114
Knox, General Henry 89
Kohen, Arnold 81

Krugman, Paul 14
Kuwait 47

Labour Party 28, 29, 109, 110
Lanchester, John 17
language 58–9, 61, 68n31, 91–3, 95 see also
    linguistics
Latin America 78–9, 111–12, 116, 117
Leahy Law 118
Lee, Sir David 49
Lees, RB 95
The Left 28
Liberty (charity) 20–1
Liebknecht, Karl 103
Lightman, Alan 10
Lincoln Lab 115
linguistics
    Allott on ROI 41
    Chomsky on Knight 90–5, 97
    Knight on ROI 54, 58, 61, 63, 68n31
    publication of ROI x
Lippmann, Walter 77
Locke, Bill 54
Lodge, Milton 35
Lukoff, F 95
Luria, Salvador 95, 114
Luxemburg, Rosa 103, 114
Lyft 23n18
lying 41n3, 7, 11, 16–17

Macdonald, Dwight 8, 30, 45, 71
MacDonald, Gordon 93
machine language 58–9, 68n31, 95
machine translation (MT) 53, 54, 95
Major, John 48
Marcuse, Herbert 77
Margalit, Yotam 41
Marx, Karl 26, 83
Massachusetts Institute of Technology
    (MIT)
    Chomsky on Allott 81
    Chomsky on historical context of ROI 6
    Chomsky on Knight 91–3, 95–8
    Knight on ROI 53–8, 59–61, 62–3, 67n7,
        68n24
    MIT campus 65, 96, 115–16
    UCL conference Q&A 104, 112, 114–16,
        119
Matthews, GH 95
May, Theresa 11
McCormack, James 53, 58–61, 66
McNamara, Robert 55, 58, 64, 98, 99
McNamara Line 55, 58
media
    Allott on ROI 38
    Chomsky commentaries x, 78, 82, 89
    Murray on ROI 73–4

and political thought 73–4, 109
Rai on ROI 45, 50–1
Smith and Smith on ROI 11, 16
social media 16–17, 119
UCL conference Q&A 103–4, 109, 110,
   119–20
Walker on ROI 28
Mencken, HL 80
Mercier, Hugo 42n20
migration 18, 20
military work
   Chomsky on Knight 90–1, 92–7
   Knight on ROI 54–5, 59–61, 62–3
   UCL conference Q&A 115–16
Mill, James 4n5
Mill, John Stuart 3, 4n5, 4n7, 106–7
missile gap 55, 98, 99, 101n43
MIT *see* Massachusetts Institute of
   Technology
MITRE Corporation 58–9, 60, 93, 94
MMR vaccine 24n32
Momentum 29
Morrison, Philip 98
Mosaic (journal) 5, 6
Murray, Craig
   Chomsky commentary on 86–90
   on ROI 9, 71–4
   UCL conference xin 3

Nader, Ralph 77
Nagel, Thomas 13
Nakata, Hiroyuki 41
Nasser, Gamal Abdel 47
National Rifle Association (NRA) 11, 23n14
National Security Agency (NSA) 7
Nazism 89, 111
neoliberalism 83, 90, 109, 111, 116
Netanyahu, Benjamin 73
net neutrality 119–20
New York Review of Books 6, 62
Nichols, Tom 14, 24n29, 24n34
Nixon, Richard 63, 85
'no platforming' 14, 24n27
NRA (National Rifle Association) 11, 23n14
NSA (National Security Agency) 7
nuclear weapons
   Chomsky commentaries 84–6, 96
   Knight on ROI 54–8, 61, 63
   Murray on ROI 72–3
   Rai on ROI 45–51
   UCL conference Q&A 104, 105
   Walker on ROI 27
Nyhan, Brendan 36

Obama, Barack 71, 100n24, 116, 117
The Old Mole (newspaper) 56
opium trade 107

Oppenheimer, Robert *66*
Orwell, George 14, 43n28

Palestinians 73, 108, 117, 119
Parini, Jay 1
Partee, Barbara 58
Partial Test Ban Treaty 98
Pentagon 47, 53–7, 67n7, 112
Pentagon Papers 47
Penzeys Spice Company 12
people of colour 9, 19, 26, 28–30, 108, 111
Podemos 112
Polaris missile system 55, 67n10
political correctness 14, 27
politics
   Allott on ROI 33–9
   Chomsky on Allott 82, 83–4
   Knight on ROI 63
   and media 73–4, 109
   Murray on ROI 73–4
   UCL conference Q&A 109, 110
populism 27
post truth 13
Pounds Commission report 68n24, 115
Powell, Lewis 77
Powell Memorandum 77–8
power 18, 28, 112–14, 119, 120
pragmatics 41
Presbyterian Church 117
press 45, 82 *see also* media
'Prevent' strategy 20, 25n52
propaganda model 45–6, 50, 84
prophets 113
public intellectuals 3, 72–3
Pugwash 104

racism 28
Rai, Milan
   Chomsky commentary on 84–6
   on ROI xin 3, 45–52
Reagan, Ronald 82, 87, 90, 111
recency effect 34
Redlawsk, David 36, 40
refugees 104, 110
Reifler, Jason 36
Republican Party 82, 105, 117
Requiem for the American Dream (Chomsky)
   19
Research Lab of Electronics (RLE) 6, 53, 54,
   95-7
RESIST 6, 96
resistance organisations 6, 96–7, 115, 119
'The Responsibility of Intellectuals' (ROI)
   (Chomsky)
   Allott on 1–4, 32–44
   Chomsky commentaries 75–101
   Chomsky on historical context 5–6

Knight on 53–70
Murray on 71–4
publication of x, 5–6, 60
Rai on 45–52
Smith and Smith on 7–25
Walker on 26–31
'The Responsibility of Intellectuals – 50 Years
    On' conference (UCL conference) xin3, 5,
    75, 102–20
'The Responsibility of Peoples' (Macdonald)
    30
Reston, James 89
Rielly, John 80
Rifkind, Malcolm 50
RLE see Research Lab of Electronics
Roberts, Andrew 72
ROI see 'The Responsibility of Intellectuals'
    (Chomsky)
Rostow, Walt 53, 68n47, 114
Russell, Bertrand 72, 103, 114
Russia 71–2, 78–9

SAGE (Semi-Automatic Ground Environment)
    air defense system 64
Said, Edward 27
Sanders, Bernie 82, 83, 109–10, 112
Schlesinger, Arthur 2
Singapore 48, 49
SLAPPs see Strategic Lawsuits against Public
    Participation
slavery 26, 108
Smith, Amahl
    Chomsky commentary on 76–80
    on ROI 7–25
Smith, Edward 35
Smith, Neil
    Chomsky commentary on 76–80
    on ROI 7–25
Snowden, Edward 7
social media 16–17, 119
South America 116
Soviet Union 46, 55, 57, 71, 78–9
Spain 112
Sperber, Dan 42n20
Starkey, David 72
Steiner, George 22, 62
STRATCOM (US Strategic Command) 84–5
Strategic Lawsuits against Public Participation
    (SLAPPs) 12
Straw, Jack 73
student movement 60, 63, 114–15
subjectivism 24n24
Supreme Court 12, 82
Syria 105

Taber, Charles 35
taxation 22, 82–3

Taylor, AJP 72
tenure 9, 72, 90
terrorism 20, 74, 87, 114
Thatcher, Margaret 83, 90, 111
think tanks 17, 24n29
Tosh, Peter 26, 30, 75
Trident nuclear weapons system 50
Trilateral Commission 76–7, 78
Trump, Donald
    Chomsky commentaries 83, 86
    ROI reflections 7, 12–15, 26, 63, 71
    UCL conference Q&A 102–5, 110, 116, 117,
        120
truth
    Allott on ROI 1, 2, 32–3, 37, 40–1
    Chomsky on Allott 81
    Knight on ROI 63
    Murray on ROI 73
    Smith and Smith on ROI 7–9, 10–19, 21
    Walker on ROI 27
Turing, Alan 89

Uber 12, 23n18
UCL conference see 'The Responsibility of
    Intellectuals – 50 Years On' conference
Union of Concerned Scientists 104, 115
United Kingdom (UK) see Britain
United Nations (UN) 85, 116
United States (US)
    Chomsky commentaries 78–9, 80, 84–5
    ROI reflections 2, 26–7, 47, 63
    UCL conference Q&A 102–3, 107, 109, 111,
        116–19
universal healthcare 39
universities 8, 9, 23n8, 27, 29, 72, 90
Uzbekistan 86

Varoufakis, Yanis 112
V-bombers 48, 49
Verrier, Anthony 47
Viertel, John 95
Vietnam War
    Allott on ROI 37
    Chomsky commentaries 80, 81, 87–9, 91,
        96
    Knight on ROI 53, 55, 58–60, 62
    publication of ROI x, 5
    Rai on ROI 47
    UCL conference Q&A 116
    Walker on ROI 26
voting behaviour 18, 33–6, 39, 40, 81, 82

Wakefield, Andrew 24n32
Walker, Jackie
    Chomsky commentary on 75
    on ROI 9, 26–31
    UCL conference xin 3, 108–9

Washington Consensus 111
wealth 83, 111, 113
Wiesner, Jerome 53–6, 58, *64*, 67n10, 97–9,
    101n43, 114
Wilson, Woodrow 103
women's rights 14, 18, 89

Yehoshua Bar-Hillel 54, 95
Yngve, Victor 95
Young, Hugo 48

Zinn, Howard 19
Zola, Émile 102

CPSIA information can be obtained
at www.ICGtesting.com
Printed in the USA
BVHW042129100320
574672BV00004B/43